On the Wings of a Butterfly

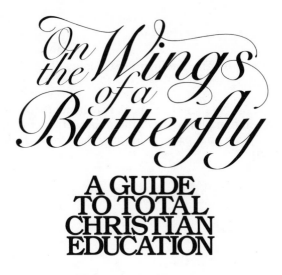

A GUIDE TO TOTAL CHRISTIAN EDUCATION

Shirley J. Heckman

The Brethren Press, Elgin, Illinois

ON THE WINGS OF A BUTTERFLY

Copyright © 1981, by The Brethren Press, Elgin, Ill.

Cover design by Rich Nickel
Illustrated by Anita Heckman and Ken Stanley

Library of Congress Cataloging in Publication Data

Heckman, Shirley J   1928-
    On the wings of a butterfly.

    1.   Christian education.   I.   Title.
BV1471.2.H398   207   80-26406
ISBN 0-87178-669-9

Published by The Brethren Press, Elgin, Illinois 60120
Printed in the United States of America

CONTENTS

FOREWORD

In 1965, Kendig B. Cully put together a book entitled, *The Search for a Christian Education — Since 1940* (Philadelphia: Westminster Press, 1965). The book was necessary because Christian education thinking had been changing swiftly and basically in the dozen or so years that he surveyed. Theological norms had been altered, educational views had shifted, and Christian education had responded in a variety of ways. Not that what was being *thought* made that much difference in what was *done*. Except as the new theological norms and educational views were embodied in new curriculums, they had little impact on education in particular congregations — even then there was a tendency to use the new plans in old ways.

The book, however, served (and continues to serve) as a symbol of the fact that Christian education is responsive to changes that take place in the church and in the world, and that it is of necessity in process of searching for direction in light of those changes. Direction-finding is essential to it.

In the last few years the concerns, fears, possibilities, and resources with which human life has had to deal have increased so fast and so enormously that the search for a Christian education today is like trying to make order out of an explosion. It is sometimes heartening, sometimes challenging, sometimes pathetic, and sometimes ludicrous to watch the church trying to identify the problems it faces internally and in society and culture, to understand those problems, and to try to figure out what to say and do about them. The task of Christian education in relation to such change is so to educate that persons will develop the knowledge, commitments, and skills to make those identifications, come to those understandings, and to have the craft, the wisdom, and the will to speak and act effectively.

Some Christian educators today seem to see that as the one and only task of Christian education, as if somehow the need for strength in the branches of a tree were justification for ignoring its roots and its trunk. They would put aside the Bible, theology, worship, and evangelism, and so define mission that it would concern itself only with the need for social justice.

Some, on the other hand, would do the same in the interests of self-fulfillment and good personal relationships, making church, society, and family subservient to the individual.

No such arbitrary limitations, however well-intentioned, will serve Christian education's purposes today. What is needed is full concern for the gospel and the church, for society and culture, for the personal *and* the corporate self, and for the means of communication, those varieties of "languages" in which people hear and, having heard, speak with others and with God.

Today's Christian education literature tends to reflect the more limited concerns. But there is hope, and some solid evidence, that it is beginning to take account of the whole necessary range of related factors. Shirley Heckman's present book is part of that solid evidence.

What she is after is a renewed and faithful church. But she does not narrow it down to one or two factors, but lets it explode as in reality it is exploding. Is all of this Christian education? The key is found in the chapter that she calls "Life Is Our Teacher." If we learn from all of life, as she maintains, and if all of life is to be Christian, then Christian education is as broad as she makes it in this book.

The method is to let life speak—in the home, in the village or city, in the congregation, on the job, across the generations—and as life speaks, to listen, to ponder, to share, to decide, and to act. In a sense it is all quite tentative, because listening to life is of necessity to remain open to change. But it also has its stabilities—the Bible, the gospel, the church, the many-generationed community of faith.

It was the anthropologist Laura Thompson who stressed the total ecology of the human, seeing the whole human community as a system made up of interacting elements—society, culture, the physical world, the body, the personality, symbols, values, codes—that are themselves systems. The whole thing is in process of becoming, sometimes in the direction of order, sometimes toward turbulence. When headed toward turbulence, the human community has ways of trying to reverse direction and move again toward order.

Heckman's book has brought Thompson's work vividly to mind, with new meaning for Christian education, for here is Christian education interpreted as a kind of ecology of the spirit. All these bewildering elements *are* necessary parts of the picture—or better, parts of the system. Each has its own life, its own relationships, its own dynamics. Yet all belong together because they are parts of an interacting whole with its own life, relationships, and dynamics. Does it seem to be headed toward turbulence? It has its possibilities for self-correction and its potential for reestablishing order.

Another way to put it is that we have here a rich mosaic of the reality and potential of Christian human experience, whose theme is the myriad ways in which we support, correct, and enrich one another through education in the home, congregation, and community, whether planned or unplanned.

Some may complain here of a lack of central attention to theology. Admittedly, Heckman does not overdo theological talk in this book. While one does get the sense of firm theological assumptions, they are seldom articulated and never argued. Heckman seems to have more of a sense of common grace than of special grace, although the latter is clearly assumed, and that sense of common grace broadens her sympathies and interests in a way that is unusual among Christian educators and that would be unlikely in the more specifically theologically oriented.

Read the *whole* book first. It may be bewildering because there is so much to it. It may be deceptive, because it seems so simple, so personal, and so human — basically just ordinary stories about ordinary people, some interpretation of those stories in concrete terms, and some talk about how it is in the family, the congregation, and the community.

But read it thoroughly, and then ponder it, analyze it, weigh what it says. Share it with other people whose experience and wisdom you value, and do so even before you feel that you understand it.

Then reconstruct it. Put it together for yourself. What stories do you have to tell? What do they mean theologically and educationally? Out of this reconstruction a new Christian education may emerge for you. You will have joined in the search for a Christian education and found a direction for it today. Then you, like Shirley Heckman, will be ready to tell your story of the ecology of the spirit. And this time it will make a difference — thought will lead to action, and action back to productive and reproductive thought.

D. Campbell Wyckoff
Princeton Theological Seminary
Princeton, New Jersey

INTRODUCTION

A Dream for the Church and the World

I have a dream.

It is a dream deeply rooted in the Christian faith.

I have a dream that one day the church will rise up and live out the true meaning of its gospel — love of God and neighbor as they confront us in Jesus Christ.

I have a dream that one day all people everywhere will have the possibility of living fully human lives.

I have a dream that the Christian church through its congregations around the world will have been an effective agent in bringing to reality that possibility.

This is the faith out of which I work.

Together with a faith like this, we shall be able to hue out of the reality given to us as a gift by God a new church that will enable that new world to be.

With this faith, we will be able to work together, to pray together, to struggle together, to do whatever is necessary together, knowing that love and justice will triumph.

With this faith, we will be able to share out of our abundance of the world's goods with those who starve and die, because we know that the death of any human on earth diminishes us all.

(Composed with gratitude to Martin Luther King, Jr., for his style of dream sharing.)

That dream, that faith is what this book is about. The book is shared out of a conviction that we must radically change our ways of living in order that we may participate with God in creating the new world that is intended to be. A task of the church is to make people whole. We are called to be disciples and to make disciples. In this book are shared stories, ideas and suggestions about ways of living together in the congregation and its households, so that out of their faith as Christians, people can create their own life-nurturing, life-sustaining dreams.

The stories are true. That is, they are taken from life experiences. In those which have not been checked with the participants, the names have sometimes been changed. Those who actually lived through the experiences described would probably tell them differently.

My decision to tell stories of our own family experiences has provided several occasions in which our conversations have been rehearsals of the experiences in the stories. In a sense, with our telling and retelling of the stories, we have recreated our past in helpful ways. Henri Nouwen in his book, *The Living Reminder: Service and Prayer in Memory of Jesus Christ,* calls us to recall our pasts in order that the wounds that are nearly forgotten but still influencing us can be healed.

Ideas, concepts, images, values are shared in these pages about the struggle to be faithful to our call to be Christian, about being a family, about being the church. They are not intended to be dogmatic or statements of truth in any ultimate sense, although sometimes they may sound that way. The ideas and understandings are simply reflections about the way life appears to be from the vantage point of one human being. They are limited because they are only one person's point of view.

What is shared here is tentative, because the ideas, understandings and convictions have developed over a period of time and are likely to change again in the future. A friend who has written several books told me that it is dangerous to write down what you believe because people stereotype you with those ideas since they are in print. Actually, in the process of writing them they change their shape and open up possibilities for future new understandings.

The suggestions for activities, for thought or discussion are offered as possibilities for your own work in the areas being considered. Although some of the suggested activities could be done by an individual alone, they are likely to be more effective if done with at least one other person. The human relationships thus involved are an important ingredient in the learning process.

It is assumed that most of the people reading this book will be involved in a congregation and participating, or able to participate, in the ongoing life and work of a congregation. The stories, ideas and suggestions about family life are shared in the hope of stimulating people in congregations to experiment with their own lives and to share about that experimentation in groups that can nurture growth. It is difficult, if not impossible, for an individual to be a Christian alone. Similarly, it may be difficult, maybe even impossible, for a family to maintain itself as a household of faith outside of a group that holds the family members accountable in nurturing ways. For Christians, community is not just an interesting idea or a good feeling to be created. It is an essential dimension in our being Christian.

In this book, the aim of education and nurture in the congregation and its households is to help people of all ages 1) to develop and maintain a linkage with the past, 2) to anticipate the future, and 3) to participate responsibly in decision-making about their lives in the present.

There are three sections of the book: the contexts for education and nurture, the people involved, and some critical issues in education and nurture. Throughout, the viewpoint of a Christian is assumed. Those of us who call ourselves Christian necessarily look at the world differently than those who do not. That perspective of faith is basic to and permeates the content of this book.

I. Contexts for Education and Nurture

Because the word "church" has so many meanings, it is necessary to establish a common image and understanding of what is meant when the word is used in this book. Just such an image and understanding is shared in Chapter One. After the description of the church, it is possible to move on to the other contexts within which nurture and education happen in congregations and households. Those contexts are time, space and wholeness.

The basic presupposition of Chapter Two is that change is universal. The theological basis for that presupposition is that God the Creator continues to create and that the universe is therefore dynamic and not static. Some of the shifts in our world since the beginning of the twentieth century are described.

The globe as the arena in which Christians are called to be in mission is the focus of Chapter Three. In the language of the faith, we can say that God created all of the earth and all that is therein. Therefore, as Christians we know that anything less than the globe is too small a territory for our witness and ministry.

Wholeness as a theological concept is the basis for Chapter Four's discussion of the fact that all of life educates us. We are whole beings who reflect the holiness — wholeness — of God. That educational dimensions are present in all of life and thus also in the whole of congregational life is the conviction developed in this chapter.

II. People of our Congregations and Households

Those of us who work to educate and nurture others must take account of both the contexts in which we live and the demands of the gospel. Attention must also be paid to the people involved with us. This section discusses people from several points of view.

The lifestyle of people of faith is the focal point for Chapter Five. A description of what it might be to live in, but not of, the world is given in abstract terms showing the paradoxes within which we must stand as Christians. A story is told of a man and a woman whose lives manifest the qualities in that description. The dreams and visions that enable us to live life in such a way are considered in the last part of the chapter.

In each of our congregations, people live in many kinds of households. Not only that, people are all different and they change as they grow through the years. Chapter Six deals with these issues in addition to providing an example of how one congregation grouped their diverse people for learning in the church.

Children in worship, children and death, and children and evangelism are the concerns in Chapter Seven. These three concerns are related directly to the three-part aim for education stated above: helping people relate to the past, the future, and the present. Children need to participate with the rest of the congregation in worship. Worship is one of the ways in which people maintain their linkage with the past. Likewise, learning about death within a context that is Christian is a crucial dimension of a child's life. Our understandings about death have to do not only with the future but also with the present.

In the section about evangelism and children, one issue involved is how the decision to become a member of the congregation enables rather than deters the responsible participation of children. That decision requires maturity enough to see the connections of the present with the past and the future.

Other issues related to the nurture of children might have been considered but these are most important to the understandings in this book about the faith, about people and how they grow, and about the church.

III. Critical Issues in Education and Nurture

Chapter Eight on ways of teaching begins with stories of three situations in which learning appeared to have taken place. Then, the ingredients of learning for a wholistic approach are identified. The descriptions of people from Chapter Six are used to suggest some teaching approaches for people of different ages.

A critical issue in both households and congregations is organizing to get the work done that is necessary to maintain those institutions. The story at the beginning of Chapter Nine tells how one family organized itself so all participated in decision-making, doing the work and celebrating its life together. Questions are raised about who does what in the households of the congregation. Illustrations of similar activity in the congregation are shared in two stories about recruiting, training, and supporting teachers. Ideas related to those same tasks are suggested.

Stories about decision-making and planning make up Chapter Ten. One is an individual's story, another that of a family. Two others are stories about congregational groups making decisions and doing planning. The chapter closes with a call to us to plan for the future so that our children's children will have food.

I.
Contexts For Education and Nurture

CHAPTER ONE

On the Wings
of a Butterfly

An Overview

One of the issues in human communication is that we carry different pictures in our heads about the same words. The word "church" has many meanings. A common understanding of the word and the concept of "church" is basic to what follows in the rest of the book. Rather than trying to define the word, let us instead consider an image, a description of the church.

The diagram below is one image of what the church is:

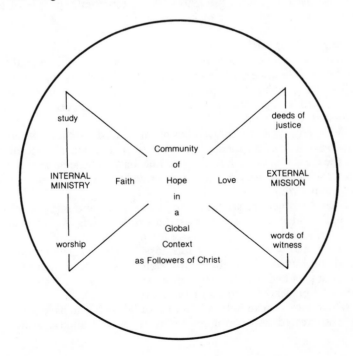

You can see that it is a butterfly in a circle. The butterfly has long been a symbol for the new being, the resurrected one. The circle has been a symbol for wholeness, for the universality of God. As we become new persons in Christ, the resurrected One, we participate in the community with other resurrected ones similarly aflame with the faith. As the community of the faithful, we can bring into being new realms of possibility for all people everywhere in the world.

Faith, Hope, Love

Almost everyone assumes some basis of faith, hopes in some kind of future, loves and is loved. That is true unless those life-responses have been destroyed by life's experiences. We are naturally people of faith, people of hope, and people of love.

We are people of faith

We cash checks. We drive through green lights and generally stop for red ones. We share confidences with each other. We send our children to school trusting that other people will teach them. We believe some of what we read in the newspaper, hear on the radio, see on the television. We tend to trust people.

We even have faith in machines of many kinds — that is, we are willing to bet our lives on them. We travel in planes, trains, automobiles. After the crash of a DC-10, some of us may have so little faith in that particular machine that we are unwilling to ride in a DC-10 anymore, but we do not quit flying.

Society's structures are based on both explicit and implicit trust, on open and hidden faith, on obvious and subtle beliefs. Try to imagine a society without such faith, such trust. It would be impossible.

Many, maybe even most, people appear to have faith in some power beyond the human. Even those who claim not to have such faith may swear at or plead with such a being or power. Our cries of despair or great joy may be prayers of petition or praise.

What does it mean to be a Christian of faith? It is to have faith in the God who created and continues to create us and all the world. It is acknowledging the Christ as our Redeemer and deciding to follow the example provided to us by Jesus. It is to know the dynamic, loving, caring presence of the Spirit who sustains us in our daily existence.

We are people of hope
In casual conversations people can be heard to make all kinds of "if only . . . then" statements of hope:

If only the sun would shine, then . . .

If only the test is not too hard, then . . .

If only my child would get well, then . . .

Hoping is a natural part of life. Everyone in the world shares the same basic hopes. We hope to survive, to have enough to sustain ourselves, to love and be loved, to have a life with meaning. Deep within each of us is a flame of hope that lights our path through life. In times of trouble or despair the flame flickers and almost dies. The decision to stay alive another day is a demonstration of that hope.

The hope of the Christian adds a different quality to life. Our hope is based in the reality of God the Sustainer. God reigns — in this world as well as in any other worlds — is the statement of faith out of which our hope flows. As Christians we live in hope, because we know that God will sustain us in this present moment given to us as a gift. We also expend our lives, enabled by our hope that God's realm will be known by all on earth.

We are also people of love
To be human is to care and to be wanted. We love. We are loved, if we are lucky ones. Almost all of us care about those who love us. We yearn that those we love will know themselves to be loved.

Again, the quality of love for the Christian is different. We know ourselves to be called to a particular ministry and mission within a global context. Jesus as our example has shown us what it means to love. It is to be called to lives of sacrificial service. We are called to live on behalf of "the least of these." We are called to go to the ends of the earth throughout all of our years to witness to the truth that out of death comes life, that in our giving we receive. We are challenged to recognize the space in which we live as the portion of the earth to which we are called to be in particular ministry and mission.

Internal Ministry
Look again at the diagram on page 19. The left wing of the butterfly is labeled "INTERNAL MINISTRY" with one tip being "study" and the

other "worship." Our planned experiences of study and worship must be consistent with each other. They must flow out of the life of the community and be that which enables the participants to go forth again in mission.

Study

Our planned ministries of study can help us remember who we are and whose we are. We can plan for occasions in which to share God's story as told in the Bible and experienced in our lives. We can consider how our stories reflect that one story.

The one story the Bible tells is that God created and continues to create us and all the earth. God loves us. God knows when we turn away from and refuse to live out of the grace so freely available to us. God accepts us just as we are, forgives us and gives us courage for the struggle to be faithful.

The teaching/learning experiences we plan in our congregations can provide opportunities for people to learn and relearn that one story. They can hear about the lives and witness of people of faith. They can share together their own struggles to be faithful.

Worship

The encounter with God, with the mystery that life is, comes in the midst of daily life. It happens when we look into the eyes of another human being, when we see the suffering of those in pain, when we see the joy in a job well done, when we experience ourselves as cut off and alone, when somehow from somewhere we get the courage to continue in life.

Worship is a dramatic act in which we rehearse how life is for us and how salvation has come to us. The rehearsal of life and of salvation happens in the same activities. The first act of worship is confession. I look at my own life and confess the pain, the selfishness and the mysterious depths of my own being. In worship I acknowledge who I am before God. In an attitude of humility I stand open to that life as it actually is. In terms of the salvation story, I receive the death of the Savior as having been for me. During worship, with confession come the words and experience of absolution because our God is merciful as well as just.

The second act of worship is praise. In life I experience my life as full of possibilities, my being sustained in the midst of the limitations with which we as human beings must live. With gratitude and thanksgiving I embrace that life as it is and give thanks. The salvation story is that out of death comes life. Not only does the Savior and Redeemer still live, I participate in that reality. God, the Creator, continues to form my being, my world, and all that is. I respond with joy.

The third act of worship is dedication. In the decision again to be responsible for my own life and that of my neighbor, I embrace that which I have reaffirmed as my hope and my faith. During that time of dedication, we offer prayers of petition for ourselves as the church, prayers of intercession for the pain in the world, prayers of commitment in which again we decide to live on behalf of all people everywhere. The offering of our bits of money is symbolic of our commitment of our lives to be again the people of God. We go forth from worship knowing ourselves to be always and ever with God the Sustainer.

Our times of corporate worship pick up again the themes of faith, hope and love that are basic to our understanding of ourselves as people. We do not always live out the best that we know. Human beings are like that. Many of us experience both times when we feel a part of the people of faith and times when we do not. Sometimes we are people of faith other than that of the gospel. We forget that God is in charge of the universe. We try to manage our own worlds. We try to control the lives of other people. We forget that the moment given to us to live is a gift from God that we can and often do squander. We spend our lives trying to accumulate enough of the world's good that we can be comfortable. We are like the rich fool of the New Testament story who tried to store up the good life for himself only to die before he began to live. Like that, we too often miss the "good" already present in the midst of the struggle for existence.

For all of these reasons and more, we need to have places and times for worship and a community within which such worship can happen. We come together for worship to celebrate with each other how God has acted in our lives since we last met. We come together for worship to remind ourselves that we are not alone in the world — that others who also call themselves children of God are called with us to announce the reality of God's realm everywhere for everyone on earth. We come together for worship to touch again the mystery that is constantly present with us. We celebrate the mysterious acts of God who graciously gave us the Christ.

External Mission

Our internal ministries of study and worship sustain us in faith. It is the external mission that provides the focal point for that internal ministry. Our words and our deeds demonstrate who we are and whose we are. In the diagram on page 19 the right wing of the butterfly is that demonstration of love through our deeds of justice and words of witness which is our EXTERNAL MISSION.

Both wings of the butterfly are necessary in order for it to fly. The wings must be balanced. It is impossible to imagine a butterfly otherwise, but sometimes in our churches we overemphasize one dimension of congregational life to the neglect of the other. Then we wonder why we are not those "Easter people" who live in joy.

Our love as Christians is seen in the doing of the deed of Christ—living on behalf of others a life of sacrificial service. That does not necessarily mean giving up all of what we have and/or going away to some other place on earth. It means living the life we have right now in the style of the servant rather than that of the ruler.

Our love as Christians is heard in our speaking and seen in our witnessing to the truth of the gospel. The truth is that only through dying does life come—our dying to our selfish illusions that we can direct our own lives, our dying to our self-centered individualism which puts us at the center of our own universes.

Our mission, our witness as those who live in Christ, is evident in our words and in our deeds. We are called to love others as God has loved us. One thing that means is that our words and our deeds must be consistent with each other. The message delivered in words and actions is one message. One of the phrases my mother used to say was, "Your actions speak so loud that I can't hear what you are saying."

Many of us who are concerned about the church's social witness are strangely reluctant to talk about our faith with those who are not Christians. Others of us have a burning conviction that the word of salvation must be said regardless of whether the hearers of our words are in need, in hunger or in poverty. To use again the image, in order for the butterfly to move, its wings must be balanced—up and down and across the two wings.

To claim our words and our deeds to be in the name of Christ does not make them so. "Not everyone who says to me, 'Lord, Lord,' shall enter the kingdom of heaven . . ." was the warning given by Jesus. Living faithfully is what matters more than the words that are said. Saying yes to life as it is given, refusing to live out of our illusions about life, providing possibilities in the midst of life all witness to the truth that Christ is present in the midst of such happenings.

Deeds of justice and words of witness are demonstrations of the presence of Christ. Maybe it is that we cannot identify our own actions and words as being Christian. Maybe it is only others who hear us and see us who can identify us as Christians. "See how they love one another" was a statement made by an observer rather than a participant.

Community of Christians Who Hope

The two wings of INTERNAL MINISTRY and EXTERNAL MISSION are held together in the body—the community of Christians who hope. Other agencies and institutions may have external missions—to get to the moon, to corner the market with a particular product, and so on. Others have the equivalent of an internal ministry—study and reflection on the deeper meanings of life. However, only the church is a community of people who have faith, who hope, who love in a particular style—that of the Christ.

The congregation, the community within which we live as Christians of faith and of love, is also that in which our hope as Christians is both realized and anticipated. The hope for the recognition of the reign of God in this world is both a present and a future reality. It is that which sustains us and enables us to give our energy to the present life and work of the church, knowing that God is continually creating and sustaining the world.

Some of us live as though our hope lies only in the future. Some who name the name of Christ insist that it is only some future heaven to which we can aspire. Such denial that our hope in Christ is present with us now may breed despair among us.

On the other hand, assuming that our hope in Christ is only in the present is saying that God is no longer active in the human realm. Our hope as Christians is present with us. Our hope as Christians is yet unfolding before us.

The Global Context

No one on earth can avoid having a global context in which to live. Many people act as though that were not the case. We deal with injustice on the global scale when we witness to and work against injustice in the neighborhood in which we live. We deal seriously with the hunger problem when we decide to eat less and work with others in figuring out means of distributing what is available to more people.

For the community of God's people to be faithful to the gospel, it must participate actively in that global context. It is not enough simply to consume goods that are produced all around the world or see and hear news from everywhere on earth.

God, the Creator, brought all that is into being. To be faithful to that creator God, we are obliged to relate to all of God's creation. That means living in ways that allow all people everywhere to live fully human lives. It means that we know all on earth as our brothers and sisters, not just those who happen to be like us. It means working with God in the continual creation and re-creation of the world that God's creatures and creation may live to their highest potential.

In *An Open Letter: The Public and Its Education,* a committee of people from the United Presbyterian Church in the USA and the Presbyterian Church in the United States, in 1969, spoke of this matter of human solidarity with these words:

> In the Christian tradition at its best, there is a strong affirmation of a deep and powerful human commonality uniting all people, everywhere and all the time. This bond is evident in the midst of and beyond all fractures and divisions, class interests and national boundaries, color lines and religious differences. It is the gift of God, inherent in creation and confirmed in Jesus Christ.
>
> In the Christ event, the issue of human solidarity was settled once and for all. We believe it is a given reality, whether it is recognized and honored. Our solidarity, rooted as it is in God's action is both an inviolable inheritance and the promise of the future. It is the solidarity, the commonality of persons, not the togetherness of Christians or religious folk or Americans or whatever, but of all humanity, that underlies the public.

As Followers of Christ

The last phrase from the diagram on page 19 is "as followers of Christ." It is necessary because we as the church are not just people of faith, hope and love who know ourselves to be in community, living in a global context with an internal ministry and an external mission. We are also, first, followers of Christ.

In the Old Testament, the covenant happening occurred among a particular people who were called out of Egypt to be faithful within a limited context (according to the Christian's view of life). Those of us who decide to believe in and follow Jesus are a called-out people with a ministry and mission in the whole world.

The image, then, of the butterfly in the circle can remind us that we are indeed resurrected ones, who each day receive from the hand of God another time in which to be faithful, hoping, loving people called to a ministry of study and worship so our deeds of justice and words of witness may be reflections of God's glory on earth. And to be the church is to be in community with others who understand themselves to be similarly renewed and called.

CHAPTER TWO

The Only Sure
Thing is Change

An Overview

That our lives change with added years and experience is commonplace information. Much of what we have done in the past in our congregations and households has seemed to be that which assumed that change does not happen, that the way it was yesterday is the way it is today and will be tomorrow.

That change is universal is the basic understanding of this chapter. The theological basis for that understanding is that God the Creator continues to create and that the universe is therefore dynamic and not static. As the beginning point for the discussion of change, the story is told of the early years of my mother's life in Iowa and southern Montana. She was born in 1901, so in her lifetime amazing changes have occurred in every dimension of the life she describes.

The discussion of shifts since the beginning of the twentieth century starts with a look at some of the responses to the change in our scientific sense of ourselves. The next shift described is that from our being people with a rural mindset to those with a cosmopolitan one, regardless of whether we might live in the city or the country. The third shift delineated is that of living in an age of plenty to now being in an age of less.

Shifts have occurred in our religious lives that parallel those in the political, cultural and economic dimensions of life. The questions that are part of our being religious include how we encounter the divine, what response we make to that encounter, where the struggle for faith happens and where our sense of the truth comes from. The final section of the chapter considers these questions.

My mother was given the name Emogene. She did not like the way her name was spelled so she changed to Imogene when she was a teenager. Her family still called her Emma. She was born on a farm in the section of Delaware County, Iowa, that was called Poverty Hollow. Her uncle told her that it was a snowy night in September, 1901, when she was born. She shares her memories of life in the early years of the century with these words:

When I was young, we really did not know that we were deprived. We did not have much money. We did have nuts, berries and fruit growing wild around the place which were ours just for the effort of picking them.

We cracked black walnuts using a rock for a hammer and a horseshoe nail for a pick. Papa took me for a fast ride on a handsled down a steep slope. I let loose but he held me in so I did not fall out. It was scary but fun.

Grandad Mast lived a few miles from our place. I remember sitting on his lap, sewing a button on his shirt. One time he spilled hot coffee on my arm. He felt terrible but it was not much of a burn.

I helped in the blacksmith shop across the road from our house when I was a child. I remember bolting the tires back on the buggy wheels after Papa had set them right. He and I were in the blacksmith shop when they came to tell us that my youngest brother, Harrison, was born.

In early 1909 when I was about eight years old, Papa heard about the Homestead Act. He went to Montana with Mama's brother, Asa. They each filed for 160 acres about seven miles from the town of Lavina. Later my Grandma Friend also filed for a piece of land.

Papa and Uncle Asa built houses on both homesteads. Each had a basement and was sixteen feet square and a story and a half high. They were not finished on the inside but they were ready for the families to move into. Uncle Asa had four children in his family. We had seven in ours.

When we moved from Iowa, everything was put into a freight car. We took along a small well-drilling rig, farm machines and furniture for the two households. We also had chickens, three cows and three horses. While we were still on the way from Iowa to Montana one of the mares gave birth to a colt which we had to bottle feed.

On our first day in Montana, I remember watching a sheepherder drive past with a big flock of sheep. One of my other memories of that day was of a beautiful yellow rose-like flower. I squatted down to look closer at the flower and when someone bumped me, I landed in a big bed of cactus.

Papa gave land on the corner of the homestead for a school. All the neighbors helped to build the one-room schoolhouse which was made of logs. I started school there in the third grade. Mama had been a school teacher. She thought it better for the children not to go to school too young and had taught us at home.

My older brother who we called Bill also filed for a homestead. So did my Grandma Mast when she came to live with us. Grandad Mast had died just before we moved from Iowa in 1909. Grandma Mast came to visit us in Montana early in 1910. So she was with us when typhoid fever struck our family.

The source for the typhoid fever was never found by the health people. None of the neighbors had it. It happened only in our family. I was sent away to stay with the doctor and his wife who did not have any children.

First, my sister Sylvia died. Then Mama died. Next Byron and finally Elphia died. All of them died within one month. My sister Myrtle also got sick and she spent ten days in the hospital. She showed the after-effects for the rest of her life. She was not as alert as you would have expected someone of her age to be.

The men of the two households were away a lot. They would go out to drill wells for neighbors as well as working on the crops when there were any. After Grandma Mast homesteaded six miles north, she and my younger brother spent a lot of time up there.

So my sister Myrtle and I were alone a lot but we got along all right. We took care of the livestock and kept things going. Aunt Sadie lived only a quarter of a mile away so we took our problems to her. She was a great help and comfort to us.

We raised chickens and had a garden. We canned some and dried corn out in the sun. The pigs were butchered once in a while. We kept butter by pressing white cloths on top to shut out the air. Then we would cover the butter with salt. We did the same thing with pork chops and other meats. We would cook them to the almost-done stage, then pack them tight in crocks and cover them with lard and salt.

I helped do the work in the fields. We had to watch out for rattlesnakes when shocking the grain. Myrtle and I worked in brown denim dresses until I was about seventeen years old. Then I saw an advertisement in a magazine for coveralls for women. It took some talking to convince Papa to let me order some. He thought such an outfit would not be very ladylike. He changed his mind after seeing how much better they were for the field work.

Grandma Mast sewed our clothes. Myrtle and I were not allowed to do any sewing. I did have one year of sewing in high school. I made myself a box-pleated skirt using a wool serge that really held the pleats. I had not shaped it right. It fit fine at the waist but did not have enough room for my hips. It was a beautiful skirt but I could not wear it.

We made many other mistakes. One time Grandma Mast wanted to get lice off the heads of the little chickens. She told Myrtle and me to grease their heads with a mixture of sulphur and lard. Apparently, we used too much. All of the chicks died.

We had fun much of the time. My cousins and neighbors of about my age would get together for popcorn and taffy pulls. We visited each other and explored the countryside. Some of the recreation and social activities were sponsored by the Methodist church we went to in Lavina seven miles away. Dances, box socials and other parties were held at the schoolhouse sometimes. Everyone would come. The little ones would go to sleep on the benches. We danced to the music of mouth organs, accordion and sometimes the fiddle.

In summer, we had picnics by the river where we played ball and other games. We would ride horses for distant visiting. In the winter, we would tie a rope to the sled and the saddlehorn and travel around. We made our own fun. Some of us read anything we could get our hands on.

A trip to town was an event. We would take a buggy or wagon and a team of horses. On the Fourth of July we had celebrations with bands, speakers, and a rodeo with a picnic afterward. Sometimes we had a few extra nickels to splurge on ice cream and other goodies.

I worked on the ranch for a year after finishing the eighth grade at Mountain View School. I wanted to go to high school. It was arranged for me to work for board and room through the week and every other weekend. The spring of my first year, I started living at home and riding a horse for the seven-mile trip. After that, I only stayed in town during the very severe weather. I never missed a day of school because of the weather, even when it was 40° below.

I enjoyed my school work and got good grades. I was the top student in the graduating class of ten. I got a scholarship to go to Montana State but we did not have the money for the other expenses.

The year after I graduated, Papa and some of the other homesteaders gave up their farming. Drought and low prices made it impossible for those with small farms to make a living. He and my brothers then worked at any jobs they could find.

I went to the nearby town of Roundup and began working as a nurse's aide at a hospital. When I was twenty-one, I married Gilbert Jackson. I continued to work some at the hospital until the twins we named

Helen and Henry were born a year later. When the twins were just over a year old, Helen developed pneumonia and died. A friend advised me to go back to work. So I did, taking the baby, Henry, along with me. We arranged a play space in the dining room in view of the cook. Sometimes we would take him along to the floor where we were working. He and the patients enjoyed each other.

In 1929, after the two older girls had been born, we moved to Sheridan, Wyoming, where Gilbert worked as a carpenter. Because it was a larger place, Sheridan had more to offer the growing family. It has been a good place to live near the mountains. I have been here for the more than fifty years since then.

In almost every dimension of life which my mother described about her early life, changes have occurred. Her life was very different during the first thirty years of her life than it has been in the last thirty years. Changes have occurred in how we understand life and in the ways in which we respond to life as it is now.

During the eighty years of my mother's lifetime, certain years seem to be symbolic or even actual turning points in our life as a nation. Three such years are 1917, 1945 and 1968. One way of talking about the shifts is that they were changes in our sense of the world, our sense of location in that world, and our perceptions of the abundance in that world.

From Newton to Einstein

A shift in our sense of the world happened in 1917. That year, the United States entered the war to make the world safe for democracy. The Bolshevik Revolution happened in Russia. Great Britain announced that Palestine should become a home for the Jewish people. Einstein announced his theory of relativity which changed our understanding of the physical world. No more could we believe matter and energy to be separate. We knew the world to be a unity. We could think of it literally as being a UNIverse.

It used to be that people talked of the substances of life being earth, air, fire and water. A scientific table of the elements was sufficient to describe the way the world was built. With the new physics and other sciences, we came to know the world to be relational, a relative universe. In our human relationships, also, we came to understand that we are relational beings. Each of us plays a variety of roles depending on the situation. I am wife, mother, grandmother, professional educator with multiple relationships.

In the shift from Newton to Einstein, we moved from believing the world to be static with absolute definitions and answers about how to live. We now know life to be dynamic. Life flows around and through us in a variety of ways. Change is constantly occurring at a rate we find difficult to comprehend.

We also now know in different ways the processes at work in the world. In the early times of the twentieth century, people argued about the existence of God. Debates were held to seek out basic causes. It was assumed that the universe operated out of cause and effect. Now we know it is not a simple mechanical system. We can only be predictors of the future. We can examine what has been, analyze the present, and make predictions about the future which are likely but not necessarily to happen.

In the past, some humans thought themselves to be victims of the world in which they lived. We asked questions like, "How do I adjust to the reality in which I live?" Now we know ourselves to be creators of our own universes. We ask questions like, "How do I create life and meaning given this situation?"

We have shifted from knowing ourselves as one party in a contract or covenant with God to knowing that we are co-creators with a creator God who continually re-creates us and the world anew.

During the 1920s, the country was in a strange state. My mother's decision to wear coveralls as she worked in the fields was an illustration of many other changes that came for women. Her taking her baby to work with her is a similar example. Women's suffrage was a move toward freedom. The vote for prohibition happened in the same year and was a move to try to control. The thirteen-year experiment in control did not work. It has been said that prohibition made us into a nation of lawbreakers and that we have not recovered from that even now.

World War II called the farm boys out to fight and the women into the factories to do "war work." The exploding of the bombs in Japan in 1945 brought an end to this era of our development. Whether we admitted it out loud or not, we knew then we were in the hands of a military complex which would run our lives.

From Rural to Cosmopolitan

The next segment of our developmental journey as a nation lasted from 1945 to 1968. During that time, suburbia developed; the times were good; psychology and sociology thrived; sciences became important in the schools. We moved from being a people with our roots in the country to being city folks. Even if you live fifteen miles from your nearest neighbor, television and ease of travel make you a cosmopolitan person.

The quality of our lives changed with this shift also. From her kitchen window, my mother could see broad plains with mountains in the distance. The external space was huge. But her knowledge of the world was limited to what she could find in the county newspaper. That degree of response is still normal for some people. For many of us, though, a shift happened with our internal and external space. Our living space is likely much smaller than before—a suburban lot, an apartment, a retirement trailer. At the same time, our perception of the dimensions of our life internally is vast. Through the media, our children experience all of life from all over the world before they go to kindergarten. Restaurants in New York City have menus in Spanish, Chinese and English. Many languages besides English are spoken in the public school system. We used to think that our children would likely grow up to have religious experiences similar to our own. Now we know that they are potential participants in all kinds of religious and so-called religious groups, some of which have frightening dimensions to them.

In my mother's childhood and youth, time moved at a pace that could be counted on. Life was related to the sun and to the seasons. Most people had only three decisions to make—whom to marry, where to live, and how to earn money. If the decision was not to marry, the other two still needed to be decided.

My mother had a choice of chocolate, vanilla and strawberry when she had a little bit of money to buy ice cream. Not so anymore. We have to choose among 31 or more flavors. Life is much more complicated than it used to be. The options are no longer simply *whom* to marry but include *whether* marriage is necessary in order to have a partner to satisfy sexual desires.

It might have been that in the past, members of a family lived nearby. Some families continued to live in the same house through several generations. Now we are more likely to move away from the family home than to continue to live where we were born. In one year in the fifth-sixth grade public school class I taught in a suburb of Denver, seventeen children came into my class and twenty left because their families had moved.

Similarly, following a single life-work throughout all of one's life is no longer assumed. Rather, one is likely to have more than one way of earning money. Studies have shown that people on the average change their jobs or professions every seven to ten years.

In the shift from being rural to being urban people, the quality of our relationships with other people has changed. In the country, the small town, the neighborhood, people knew each other intimately. They knew the families from which people came. When I was growing up in Sheridan, Wyoming, I was Jack the carpenter's daughter. As you shopped, you talked with the people in the store because you knew them personally.

Now many of us live in situations in which we do not know the people who live next to us. The care provided in the city is structural care. If we love our neighbors, we take care of the garbage, get rid of the dandelions in our grass, and clean snow from our walks. We may come to recognize the people in the grocery store but we are not likely to stop to chat with them for a half-hour.

The methods for identifying ourselves have changed also. One reason why we might be vaguely uneasy when we go to a family reunion or a gathering of a high school class five or twenty-five years after graduation is that none of us is the same person we used to be. When we gather on the basis of past relationships, the people we are now may not fit very well.

In the Church of the Brethren, and perhaps in other denominations, much talk is heard about who one is on the basis of past relationships, with comments like: "Where are you from?" "Who were your parents?" "Oh, you are niece, granddaughter, son of . . . " No, thank you. You cannot know me on the basis of my family or my birthplace. You would not have known them anyway.

The questions for today need to be something like: "What do you do?" "What do you intend to do and be in your lifetime?" "What dreams do you have for the church for which you are willing to spend your life energy?" Those kinds of questions point toward the future rather than the past. Who I am is more concerned with being related to the globe and its people than having been born in Musselshell County Hospital in the Gilbert and Imogene Jackson family.

From Plenty to Less

During the year 1968, several happenings pointed us toward a different perception of ourselves and our world. Some say that year can be seen as the watershed year between the Age of Plenty of the past and the Age of Less in which we now live.

The move of my mother's family from Iowa to Montana and then on to Wyoming was one of the hundreds of such migrations toward the possibility of a better life. They were some of the last who had a frontier to which to move. Each generation envisioned the possibility that life could be better for them than it had been for their parents. We lived in an age of abundance in which there would always be plenty, an age of expansion in which there was always the possibility of having more. That was never true for some in our society and it is no longer true for any of us.

Look at this list of happenings during 1968. They indicate that the world was not and never would be the same again.

Student riots and demonstrations around the world — Senegal, Ethiopia, Seoul, Warsaw and the rest of Poland, Rome and Milan, West Berlin. In Paris, the Sorbonne was closed because of student demonstrations. In Mexico City, the demonstrations continued for more than nine weeks and in one twenty-four hour period, fifteen students were killed. The United Arab Republic closed all of its universities as a control measure. The young people were refusing to be victims of the societies in which they lived.

And in the United States, it was not just the young who protested, although they did so throughout the country on campuses from Columbia in New York City to San Francisco State College as well as during the Democratic National Convention in Chicago. The assassination of Martin Luther King, Jr., in April, set off riots through the country to which federal troops were sent. Three blacks were killed in Orangeburg, S.C., during an attempt to desegregate a bowling alley. The killing of Robert Kennedy in June added to the unease and anger of the blacks, the young, the liberals.

Some of the anger of the young had to do with selective service. Benjamin Spock and four others were convicted of counseling young men to resist the draft. The Supreme Court upheld a 1965 decision that it was criminal to burn or deface a draft card. The report was released that 952 men had been convicted of violation of the Selective Service Act in 1967.

Vietnam peace talks were held intermittently while the war continued without ceasing. Nigeria destroyed Biafra during that year with the refusal to allow airlifts of food to the starving people there. The USSR invaded Czechoslovakia. The war continued in the Middle East. The U.S. Navy ship "Pueblo" was seized and the men of the "Pueblo" were not released for eleven months; then only with the admission by the United States to Korea that the ship had been where it ought not to have been. Canada sold wheat to Communist China. The United Nations General Assembly again rejected a resolution to seat Red China.

The economy world-wide was uncertain. Bank rates shifted. The United States went off the gold standard. The stock market had new records in April with the previous record having been in 1929 when the market crashed. DeGaulle announced a wage-price freeze and new budget cuts for France. Workers around the world were unwilling to live as they had and went out on strike—for instance, garbage collectors in New York City and Memphis, an eight-month nationwide copper strike in the United States, nationwide work strikes in France, a three-week postal strike in Canada, and a newspaper strike in Detroit for 267 days.

Surveyor 7, Apollo 7 and Apollo 8, as well as Russian spacecraft flights, were successful. A whole new image of the earth was provided in the picture of the earth looking like a blue marble floating in a sea of black space.

In the 1969 *Encyclopedia Britannica* (which was the source for all this data about 1968), for the first time a water pollution chart was printed among the charts and maps of the condition of the United States. In that same publication, it was reported that hunger and malnutrition was widespread in the United States.

After such a year, the universe in which we lived was different than it had been before. The image of our globe as shown in the picture of earthrise is as much of a change as the shift from understanding the world to be round instead of flat. It is a different universe we live in since 1968. The people living on that earth had demonstrated a different response than any before. They refused any longer to be victims. The dispossessed, the young, the Blacks, the workers had decided that they could move toward some control of their own destiny.

Being Religious in These Days

Out of all this has come a new internal awareness of all of life being that which calls us to respond in faith—not just that which has been labeled as religious. We have a new sense of where the meaning in our lives arises. The shifts in this dimension of our lives have come in how we encounter the divine, what response we make to that encounter, where the struggle for faith happens and where our certitude, our sense of the truth, comes from.

From the edge to the center

Many of the images that were formerly used to talk about the encounter with God placed that encounter at the edge of life. When people talked of the divine mystery in their lives, they told stories of being at summer camp, in the mountains, beside a favorite stream, at the beach. Birth and death were seen as the only times when one actually met God, and the sacraments of the church reinforced that feeling. Some people thought of God as a remote deity in some supernatural world beyond or above the one in which we live.

Our experience indeed affirms that God is present at the edges of life—like in the mountains, at the occasions of birth and death. But now we know that the encounter with God also happens in the midst of our daily lives. Whenever in life we are confronted with the reality of our human limitations, we come up against the power which Christians and some others call God. When we are confronted with the choices we have to make, with the relationships we develop, with the inescapability of our own death, we know that God is in charge of the universe. And that universe includes all of life, not just parts of it. Our times of unfaithfulness and sin are evident when we try to manage our lives and those of other people, taking on ourselves the role which only God can play.

From eternal patterns to temporal models

It used to be that our response to the God we met at the edge of life was to find out and conform to eternal patterns of what was right and wrong, good and bad, true and false. Our task as humans was to determine the right, the good, the true, and live out those patterns. We needed only to find out what was wrong, bad or false, and avoid that. Life's choices are now known not to be that simple.

We have to choose between right and right, between wrong and wrong. Having to choose between two presidential candidates, neither of whom is really acceptable, is an illustration of that dilemma. Instead of eternal patterns of truth, good, right, now we know that we live out of temporal models. We create the reality out of which we live. Change is constant. The rate of change increases. What seemed right yesterday is seen as destructive today. The development of a highway system in this country that depends on a never-ending supply of petroleum products is an example of this kind of shift.

We need now to help people learn to anticipate the future and to participate in the present. Our ways of doing that must also enable the people to maintain their continuity with the past so we are not a people without roots who wither and die. Each local situation in which we live is unique. That uniqueness forces those in that situation to create for themselves models for their life together.

From struggle with supernatural powers to natural causes

When we think of where the struggle to be faithful lies, we need to keep reminding ourselves that the struggle is with natural powers, not supernatural ones. Common religious language in the past spoke of being possessed by demons or by Satan. In the more modern understanding, aided by psychology, we speak of being controlled by that which happened to us early in our lives, of being victim to the id or the ego as though we had no power to make decisions about our own lives.

A quick look at the events of 1968 listed on pages 35-36 shows the struggles to be the result of natural powers, those which arise out of the decisions which humans make. Even when you think about pollution as being one of the issues with which we must deal today, it is clear that the problem is with the decisions which human beings make. The inhumanity and destruction of war come from human decisions. The inequity and injustice that cause world hunger are the result of decisions which human beings make individually and collectively.

From authority to authenticity

And how in the midst of such a situation does one know what the truth is? In the distant past, people may have been willing to live out of the definitions of truth which kings, priests, rulers, theologians and scholars made. These authorities may have been perceived as being somehow more divine and more close to the truth. If that was the case previously, it certainly is not true now. We have come to be skeptical that those we elect to hold high office will tell us the truth. The media makes no claim to being objective in its reporting. With the variety of points of view being delivered as the truth of the gospel, we cannot even be sure about that so-called truth. There is no way in which all of the viewpoints can be true.

We have to decide for ourselves what the truth is that we are willing to live out of. We know what feels authentic to us. We can use the critical factors which are among the gifts of God to us to determine what seems to be responsible action in the situation given. We can test our insights in communities we trust.

In our contrast of old ways with new ways of living in the world, we have talked primarily about life in the United States of America. When we expand the context to that of the globe, which the gospel compels us to do, we must consider some other factors in order to come up with a realistic picture of the world in which we live and in which we must struggle to be people of faith. Those issues will be considered in the next chapter.

CHAPTER THREE

The World is Our Classroom

An Overview

The globe as the arena in which Christians are called to be in mission is the focus of this chapter. In the language of the faith, we can say that God created all of the earth and all that is therein. Therefore, as Christians we know that anything less than the globe is too small a territory for our witness and ministry.

The story that opens this chapter describes one family's hospitality which provided the members of that family the experience of knowing people from many places around the earth. Some ideas about how to get a global picture in our congregations and households is the next part of the chapter.

In the next section entitled, "Poor Versus Rich," some ideas are shared about ways of viewing the world as whole. One step in a learning process is to become aware. Another one is knowing how to analyze the situation to which one has awakened in ways that may lead to action. The idea that we might consider the world in economic terms is presented as a means of motivating action.

In the final part of the chapter, three ways of responding to human hurt are discussed—giving direct aid, working to change unjust systems, changing lifestyle.

When Cindy answered the phone, it was obvious that she was talking to a SERVAS traveler. SERVAS is an international organization which brings together host families and visitors. It describes itself as being an open door to travelers to homes and hearts in over sixty countries.

SERVAS, which is the Esperanto word for "to serve," operates out of a statement by M. K. Gandhi: "With every true friendship, we build more firmly the foundation on which the peace of the whole world rests." (For more information about SERVAS, write to United States SERVAS Committee, Inc., 11 John Street, Room 406, New York City, New York, 10038, phone 212-267-0252.)

Cindy's questions and statements in the conversation were: "Tell me what you are wearing. Which way is the door of the bus station from the phone where you are talking? What is the phone number there? I'll call you back within twenty minutes."

A SERVAS traveler from somewhere in the world had arrived at one of the two bus stations in Denver. The question about what the person was wearing was to help the one doing the pickup to identify who they were to meet. The question about the direction of the door indicated which of the two bus stations the call was made from. Sometimes the questions were in a different order. Usually people were asked to spell their names, also.

Since Cindy knew that her mother was not within reach by phone, she called her dad's office to tell him about the visitor. They agreed on the time at which he would be at the bus station to pick up the traveler on the way home from work in the late afternoon. She then called the traveler back to tell the person the kind of car her dad drove and the time at which he would come by the bus station.

If the person was from India or Pakistan or another country where many people are vegetarian, the one preparing the evening meal would make it a vegetarian one—just in case. A section of the freezer was set aside for storage of bread and other staples acceptable to vegetarians. Fortunately, the family liked lentil soup and macaroni and cheese.

The two girls took turns living in the upstairs bedroom knowing that when guests came that bedroom became the guest room. It had to be ready for such a change. The current resident of the bedroom would move in with her sister in the basement bedroom for the duration of the visit.

Guests came quite often. The family had decided that they did not need any notice before receiving overnight guests. SERVAS provides lists of host families to approved travelers. In the notes by the family name was NPNR—no previous notice required.

Denver was a popular place to visit. Through the years, people came from Switzerland, Tanzania, Germany, Turkey, Israel, England, Japan, Argentina, India, Russia, Kenya, Holland.

One memorable family was that of Surjit Singh who was an architect working on the Yadvindra Colony at Patiala in the State of Punjab. Gurdip Kaur, the wife and mother, was a school teacher. Pradeep, the twelve-year-old accompanied one of the family sons to school one day. His hair—not cut because they were Sikhs—was very long and braided and piled on top of his head. Some of the students in the classroom thought he was a girl. Then he began to talk in a very deep voice and explained to them in very good English why his hair was that way. Rana, the five-year-old-daughter, was taken to the preschool attended by the youngest member of the host family. Rana was able to knit and braided everyone's hair, including her own.

Another visitor was Bernhard Vogeli. He liked traveling in SERVAS style. When he returned home, he became the Swiss secretary for SERVAS, so he interviewed prospective travelers. Everyone who came from Switzerland for five years after his visit knew him. One time two young women came from Switzerland. We mentioned having had Bernhard as a guest. One of the young women said that she was engaged to marry Bernhard. Eighteen years after his visit and fifteen years after hers, the parents of the Denver host family traveled in Switzerland where they were guests in what was then the Bernhard and Irene Vogeli family. Their ten-year-old daughter was about the age of the children of the Denver family during the earlier visits.

A Global Family

Having guests from other countries and cultures is just one of many ways of getting a sense of people from cultures other than our own. In the description of the church in Chapter One, the global context for the church's ministry and mission was stated. The sharing in each other's lives allows the possibility of knowing the fullness of God's work among us. Occasions can be provided in both the congregation and its households in which all of the people involved can affirm their dignity, distinctiveness and value. They can also learn to appreciate those qualities as present in other people.

In addition to having guests in the home, households can experiment with the language, food and games of other cultures and countries. UNICEF has a cookbook which could be used by children.

Many children and young people learn languages other than English at school. Consider encouraging the whole family to learn along with them. A day could be designated each week on which only the language being learned would be spoken.

Throughout the history of the United States and still continuing, a flow of people have come from other parts of the world to settle in this country. Some come by choice. Others are forced by circumstances to leave their homes. In most communities, recently arrived people can be welcomed into both households and congregations.

Besides becoming acquainted with people from other cultures, effort must be made in both the congregation and its households to maintain a global perspective. That is not easy. Close your eyes and think about the map which was hung in the classroom when you were in school. If you were born before 1950, and for some born after that, the world map was likely to be one in which the United States was in the center with Asia split on both sides. It is no wonder that we continue to think that the United States is the center of the universe with a natural right to anything in the world.

The kind of world map we need is one in which either the Pacific Ocean or Africa is in the center in order that Asia not be split and misshapen. One congregation decided to use such a map in this way:

A large bulletin board was placed in the fellowship hall in which people gathered between church school and worship. It looked like this:

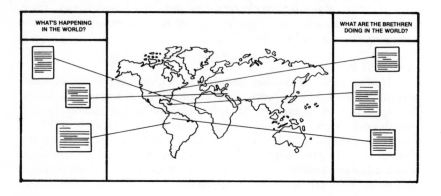

The junior high group had the task of providing clippings for the map display. Each week two of the group, instead of meeting with the rest of their church school class, looked through weekly news magazines and daily newspapers for items to put on the WHAT'S HAPPENING IN THE WORLD? side of the display.

For the WHAT ARE THE BRETHREN DOING IN THE WORLD? side, they used mailings that were sent to the pastor, bulletin inserts, the monthly denominational magazine and other interpretive pieces from the denomination's general office.

Their last task was to use a world atlas and find out where on the map to put pins in the locations of both kinds of activities. Red pins were used for the WORLD items and blue ones marked the BRETHREN activity. Then the items and the pins were hooked together with strings.

Consider putting a map of the world near the place where the family eats meals. In one family, they play a game with one person choosing a name from the map without telling the others where it is. Then the others ask questions about the location that can be answered only with YES or NO.

In another family, the conversation at the evening meal includes talking about the news of the day. Members of the family try to find items that tell of happenings in the world other than those related to war and those that occurred outside the United States.

Poor Versus Rich

Just having information about the rest of the world is not sufficient. In addition to knowing people from other countries and locations of places on maps, we need also to have ways of comprehending the situations which cause human suffering. Before we know how to act in response to suffering, we need to consider factors involved in that situation. One set of factors involved in the world today which causes untold suffering is that very few people control most of the earth's resources. Most people on earth have little with which to live and faint hope of changing that situation. For billions of people on the earth, the enemy is those of us who consume much of the world's goods and who enjoy a high standard of living. We can decide to live with less in order that some people on earth can live at all.

We need to expand our ways of thinking about the world. To think only politically is limiting. For instance, I was taught and then taught others to see the world as "democratic us" and "communist them." A diagram that held what I thought the world was looks like this:

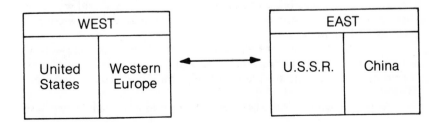

A diagram that more adequately represents the globe and illustrates more realistically the tensions in the world today looks like this:

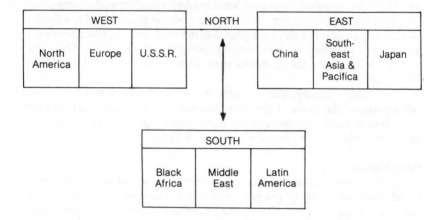

The tension is between the North (both East and West) and the South, between those who have and those who have not.

Many of us in the church identify the rich as being those other than ourselves. In relation to the globe, that is not so. Anyone who has the basic necessities of food, clothing and shelter is rich in comparison to many on earth.

For some years, we have talked about having three economic worlds on earth. We identify the advanced industrial nations with more or less capitalistic, market-oriented economies as the First World. The Second World includes the centrally planned, communist-run countries. The Third World has been identified as the developing nations.

If we could talk of the Third World as including those countries who have resources but not advanced technology, two more situations can be seen. The countries of the Fourth World would be those who have some resources and the possibility of development. The Fifth World would be those who have no resources and who are not even able to grow enough food to feed themselves.

It may be that it is not helpful to identify these "economic worlds" with nations. In every nation, including our own—in every community, including our own—are people who live in the Third, Fourth and Fifth Worlds.

As people who are called to live in this world as it really is, we have no alternative other than to consider all the people in the world as we plan for and carry out our dreams for the future.

An activity which has helped some people to begin to sense the inequities between the poor and the rich countries of the world is to play a game. At least twenty people are needed. One hundred pieces of food—like carrot sticks or celery stalks—are needed.

The figures used in the chart below are from the December 22, 1975, *Time* magazine which described the five economic worlds discussed above.

	People	Space	Products*
First World	20%	18%	53%
Second World	34%	24%	5%
Third World	16%	28%	26%
Fourth World	25%	25%	15%
Fifth World	5%	5%	1%

*Based on gross national product.

Divide up your group proportionately so that they represent the population shown above. For every twenty people have twenty 3" × 5" cards marked:
Fifth World—1; Third World—3; First World—4; Fourth World—5; Second World—7. It is helpful to have different colored cards for each of the worlds.

Divide up the space you have available by putting masking tape on the floor or separating the five spaces with chairs. If your space was square, the division would look like this:

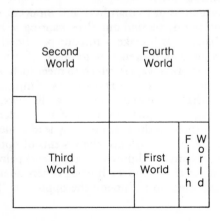

Ask the people to stand in the space allocated to the world marked on the card given them. Give each group of people the number of pieces of food listed as the percentage on the chart.

Suppose, for instance, that you have forty people participating. In the 24 percent of the area which is the land available to the Second World, 14 people would have five pieces of food. The eight people in the 18 percent of the space allocated to the First World would have 53 pieces of food. And so on.

Now the action. Ask the people with extra food to try to express their concern for those in the other worlds without sharing their food. They can ask questions about health, culture, games, music—anything except sharing the food. After a time, stop the process and talk about what happened.

As a next step in the process, try negotiation. The group that is in each world will send one person to be the negotiator for them. The five people from the five worlds will have the task of deciding how to manage an equitable distribution of the food without those who have plenty just giving directly to those who have not. The representatives can be replaced when someone else from the same world touches the representative who then returns to the assigned space. Only the five people designated can talk. One possible solution which may develop in the group is that all of the resources could be placed in a central place with each going by to pick up a fair share.

Such a game would need to be just one part of a larger program in which people might have the opportunity actually to consume less and to share more.

Response to Human Hurt

With the awareness of human hurt and innocent suffering present everywhere in the world, we find ourselves wanting to respond. When a natural disaster like an earthquake, a tornado or a flood happens and we hear about it, a natural tendency is to share of our abundance and money. We also seek other ways in which to meet such immediate needs.

When awarenesss comes to us that victims of injustice have pain and suffering as real as that of the victims of natural disasters, responding only with direct aid feels inadequate to some of us. Understanding of and identification with those in the situation may lead some of us to work at trying to change the unjust systems, the systems of oppression.

Still another response to human suffering and pain comes when we recognize ourselves as those who are hurting others directly or indirectly, when we know ourselves to be among the oppressors. Some of us then make changes in our lifestyles in order to witness with authenticity to convictions based on our faith.

Giving direct aid

We provide direct aid to those who need it by giving money, goods and services through agencies which are equipped to deliver them where needed. Some agencies involve those they serve in decision-making and administration. This provides a dignifying sense of control of one's own destiny.

That sense of dignity is diminished and the feeling of being the victim of another's charity is increased when the aid is given personally and directly. Those receiving the aid are forced to "pay" for the help by expressing gratitude or providing other expected responses directly to the giver.

If, however, aid is given in ways that those receiving it can work together with the givers in the restoration and rebuilding, the human dignity and sense of self-worth of all is enhanced.

Working to change unjust systems

Methods of nonviolent action to bring about social change include . . .

. . . protest and persuasion such as marches and protest meetings,

. . . social noncooperation like moving to another country to avoid the draft,

. . . economic noncooperation like boycotts and strikes,

. . . political noncooperation like refusal to pay taxes and nonviolent intervention like sit-ins.

A well-known example of a strike and related boycott is that of the United Farm Workers Organizing Committee. In the grape boycott in support of the strike, hundreds of people picketed, distributed materials, held conferences with owners and managers of stores, worked for national legislation and published appeals to others to support the boycott. Many people participated by refusing to buy the wine or eat the grapes.

Many of the people who participated in these and other ways were not themselves the direct victims of the oppression. They perceived the injustice, identified with the victims of it, and supported and participated with the victims who provided leadership and direction to the boycott. The victims of the injustices organized themselves and worked together in ways that enabled others to participate with them in changing the system.

Changing lifestyle

Awareness of human suffering and need for the changing of unjust systems also raises for some people the question of their own lifestyles. Suggestions about ways of changing our style of living bombard us continually, particularly through the media. Besides the pressure to consume more goods and services, we are also urged to more responsible use of energy and other conservation measures. Sometimes our lifestyle changes are forced on us through scarcity.

The question for the Christian is what values can be used as a basis for deciding among the many contradictory possibilities available to us. Doing Bible study individually and in groups as well as serious study of the global situation can provide a context for such decision-making.

It is difficult to make and maintain change in personal and family lifestyles without the support of a group who share the convictions that stimulate the desire to change. Through study, discussion, prayer and joint action, appropriate values for lifestyle decision-making can become more clear. Then, with support, it is possible for individuals, households, and congregations to reassess their values and change their priorities of time, money, and energy toward a life more consistent with the chosen values.

CHAPTER FOUR

Life is Our Teacher

An Overview

Wholeness as the theological concept is the basis of this chapter's discussion of the fact that all of life educates us. We are whole beings who reflect the holiness—wholeness—of God. That educational dimensions are present in all of life and thus also in the whole of congregational life is a conviction developed in this chapter.

The story of a young man's journey out of and back into the church is shared as an illustration of our inability to know how, when, where and in what circumstances people learn much of that out of which they live.

In the next section, some of the factors that educate us are listed. Then, some of those listed are discussed as being influential in forming values out of which we live. Some ideas are shared about how the church might respond to and/or participate in the education that happens to us. The educating forces discussed are: schools, colleges and universities; libraries, museums, voluntary associations; the mass media; and the military.

In the last part of the chapter, stories and ideas are shared that illustrate the truth that the whole congregation teaches.

John was elected chairman of the church board just before he turned twenty-nine years old. That is not surprising except to people who had known him through the years.

During his junior high years, he began to protest going to church with the family. He dropped out of church completely when he was about sixteen.

By then he had begun earning money. He bought a motorcycle over the protests of his parents. His youngest sister liked having rides behind John on it. His parents said that his grades had to stay above passing levels or the motorcycle would be taken away from him. The grades slipped. The motorcycle was locked up. He ran away from home.

He went to be with a family from the church. The adults of that family were close friends with his parents. But they also had a relationship of trust with John. At his request, they did not tell his parents where he was. Out of their concern for his parents, though, they sent a message to his mother and father through a strange grapevine that John was all right.

After his return home, his relationships with his parents, brother and two sisters got worse. He and his friends were smoking marijuana. They may have been using other drugs.

He and his friends often worked on their cars. At one time, five cars were in the yard or the garage with only the two his parents used in working order.

During his last year of high school, he was assigned to read a novel by John Steinbeck and report on it. He was intrigued by Steinbeck, read several of his books and a biography about him. He had several conversations with his mother about Steinbeck and his books but did not turn in the required report so he received a failing grade.

He and his father had little involvement with each other during his late teenage years. He did maintain a relationship with his mother. One time he decided that his mother who worked with young people should learn to listen to the music of the young rather than just tolerate it as noise. He explained to her that the words of the songs carried messages that she needed to hear. Then he invited her to let him teach her to hear the words and enjoy the music. His stereo was in his small room. He had her sit in the "right" place in the room. They listened to the record through twice, just listening. Then he gave her a copy of the words to follow as she listened the third time. Then she would listen without having the words in front of her, concentrating on hearing what was being sung. He insisted that she only needed to learn to pay attention. He was right.

One Sunday morning when he was about nineteen, he telephoned his mother at the church during the church school hour. When she answered the phone, he was crying and nearly hysterical. He was terrified that the police were going to find him and beat him up. The wife of a friend of his had just telephoned him, saying that the police had been at their house with a warrant with John's name on it but the friend's address. The police, as their custom was in those days in that city, had beat *up his friend, not believing his protests that he was not the one named on the warrant. Finally the wife was able to convince the police to look at her husband's driving license. The warrant was for the possession and sale of marijuana.*

John's mother suggested that he get dressed and come to the church which was only two blocks from their house. She said that the police would not be able to mistreat him in such a setting. She then arranged for John to have a conversation with her and his father in the church library. His father had not known until then that John was using marijuana. His father was both angry and hurt that his wife who had known for some time had not told him.

His father called a lawyer who advised the family not to return home but to come to the lawyer's office early in the afternoon. The lawyer talked with John and his parents for a while. Then he sent the parents out of the room while he arranged with John about where he could disappear. As she left the room, his mother reminded John of some families he could trust. It was arranged for the lawyer to pick up some clothes for John. His parents were asked to have the deed for the house ready for bail in case John was arrested. The lawyer did not want to leave him long in the hands of the police. The parents were told to go home and vacuum his room thoroughly. About a week later, John was able to return home. The lawyer had been able to get the warrant set aside because it had the wrong address on it.

When John was not quite twenty-one, he married a beautiful red-haired sixteen-year-old. His parents raised questions with them about their maturity. The wedding was held in the church building. Her family had not been much involved with the church and its program.

His very young wife tried to finish high school by taking night classes. He worked on varying shifts as a computer operator. He held several jobs, none of them for very long. Finally he decided to start his own business as a locksmith, at first simply operating out of a truck.

With his marriage and family, John had settled down as a responsible householder. During the first half year of their marriage, his father spent much time with the young family because John's mother and the rest of the family had moved to another state for her to take a new job. His father needed to stay in that city to fulfill work commitments before he could join those who had already moved. Since that time, the relationship between John and his father has been a helpful one for both of them.

Two children and five years later, the marriage was in trouble. They separated and finally were divorced. Primary custody of the children was with their mother.

In need of money, John requested a loan from the church credit union which his father had helped to start years before. They gave him the loan. Somewhere John had picked up the idea that you do not just take from an organization without investing some of yourself in it. He was also lonely and looking for relationships. He showed up at the January annual meeting of the credit union and allowed himself to be elected secretary. That meant that he met with three or four people from the church each month.

By that fall, he was taking his children to church school on the weekends they were with him. In response to his mother's question asking him why he would do that, he wrote that he had two good reasons.

One reason was that he remembered church school as a good experience. That surprised his mother because her memories of him in church school were different from that. She remembered his staying under the table in kindergarten when all the others would sit in a circle for the story. She remembered his father being called out of the choir to discipline him when he was in the third grade. She remembered his protests about going with the family to church. He remembered people who had cared about him. He recalled occasions on which he had fun.

The other reason for taking the children to church was even more surprising to his mother. He said that the people in that congregation had loved him all of his life and that he had not known that for a while. He wanted his children to have that possibility also.

It was not long before he began attending Sunday morning worship, church school and some of the social activities. He and a young woman fell in love and were married when he was twenty-eight years old.

That fall he began working with the stewards commission of the congregation. He took his responsibility to care for the building very seriously. His father was on the stewards commission of another congregation. The two of them had many conversations about caring for the church and its property.

When the elected members of the church board met the next June on a retreat to select officers and begin to plan for the year, John was among them. One of the items on the agenda was the selection of a person to chair the board for the next year. The man who had done that job for several years was no longer on the board. The group listed their criteria for the new chairperson and then had a time of prayer in which they sought guidance in making the decision.

After the time of silence, they began to talk about possibilities among them for doing the job. John's name was suggested. He declined, saying that he did not think he ought to do it. Then the group matched up John with their qualifications. He then agreed to do the task, asking for their help as he carried it out.

Some of the people that John claims to have known him and loved him all of his life talk about the mysterious ways in which God works, about how difficult it is to predict what will happen with people, and about how we cannot really be certain about what those we teach and nurture actually learn.

We learn and grow in the midst of living. In the ongoing flow of life, we learn — birth, death, illness, accidents, personal crisis, unemployment, close personal relationships, family breakdown, imprisonment, moving from one place to another. We learn and grow as a normal part of our lives.

The situations in which we live teach us. Economic, political and cultural factors influence our learning. The person living in the country has a different setting for learning than the one in the city. We learn from the ways in which the people around us treat us.

It is not clear when and where John learned whatever he did that was the basis for the different decisions reported and implied in the story. Where and how did he acquire the skills and sensitivity that the other members of the church board identified as desirable in one who chaired their board? And where and how did the people in the congregation learn to be the receiving and accepting ones they obviously were to affirm John in his initial moves back toward the congregation?

Many factors are obviously involved in our learning experiences. Several forces are at work in the world that educate us both consciously and unconsciously. The values, attitudes, skills, knowledge and concepts we acquire are the products of multiple forces. The Education Working Group of a program unit of the National Council of Churches, in a paper dated December 1979, listed the following as being forces that educate people in the United States:

   . . . schools, colleges, and universities,
   . . . libraries, museums, foundations and other non-traditional educating institutions,
   . . . voluntary associations like unions, fraternal organizations, professional associations, neighborhood groups,
   . . . the mass media,
   . . . the family,
   . . . the churches, synagogues and other religious communities,
   . . . business and industry,

. . . the military,
. . . international political/social bodies,
. . . alternative education experiences.

The people of the congregation and its households can be involved not only in the learning that happens in both places but they also participate in the education of the public, including themselves. Dr. Barbara Hargrove wrote a paper for the committee which made the list of educating forces about the church's educative role in society. The report was published in the Spring 1980 *UME Connexion,* a periodical of United Ministries in Education. In it, she writes:

> Organizationally the churches have an instrument of education unequalled by any institution except that of public education—if that. They have facilities and programs to educate people from birth until death, from the most elementary forms of knowledge to sophisticated graduate programs. They have programs and patterns that allow not only formal education but also learning by doing, learning within supportive human environments, learning not only through the intellect but also through the emotions. They are equipped to teach, and to teach holistically. Even that which is taught unintentionally may for that reason be more powerful in the lives of people than what is intentionally taught in the schools . . . .
>
> What the churches, like all positive educative forces, *can* do is to teach what they do know with both humility and confidence, knowing that it is a window to larger learning, to greater understanding. They can so teach and nourish people in their care that they produce a significant cadre of people who:
>
> 1) believe that there is an overall, *public* purpose for human life;
> 2) are willing to engage in the public task of seeking the specific actions required to pursue that purpose in this day and time, aware that they don't have all the answers; and
> 3) can mobilize a constituency which will support the working out of that purpose in the educative systems of the society.
>
> If Christians do believe that God has a plan and purpose for the corporate life of humankind, then they have an obligation to assist the society in educating its people to fulfill that purpose. They do so directly in the education of their own people to responsible participation in the public as carriers of the vision. They educate indirectly whenever their own internal life models the vision of human destiny in God, as well as through the agency of those whose experience of that corporate life in the church sends them out into public life confident of the reality of that vision.
>
> Their public pronouncements can only have the power to educate if they are backed by such evidence in everyday life of the reality of

which they speak. But if that backing is present, the churches have particular power to offer a frame of meaning and hope within which the products of all educative forces may be assimilated, utilized and directed toward positive goals for both individuals and society.

Any serious student of the Bible knows that not all learning about what it means to be faithful or not faithful happens within the congregation and its households. Jesus taught a large group gathered on a hillside, while eating, in discussions in public places, in a boat and while walking along the road, as well as in the temple as the prophets did or as the one explaining the scripture in the synagogue. Occasions for learning and teaching varied from his being alone in the desert to his being in the midst of the crowd at a wedding feast. In Jesus' time, the synagogue and the temple were not separate from the rest of life. They were an integral and important part of the culture. In our time, the congregation and its households are set in a world in which the people in them are bombarded with pressures that may not be consistent with the goals and dreams of the congregation or the household.

Randolph C. Miller in his *Christian Nurture and the Church* wrote: "Christian education is broader than the church or the family. Christians live in the world as disciples of Jesus Christ, and this is infinitely harder than expressing that discipleship in the church."

Think about the messages which come to you and others in your household and congregation. In addition to the messages which are obvious, we are influenced by much of which we are not consciously aware. We constantly have to decide among conflicting values. We make decisions without knowing what motivates us to do what we do. Change happens so quickly that what was an appropriate response yesterday may not be a responsible reaction today or tomorrow.

The Report to the Club of Rome, *No Limits To Learning,* published by Pergamon Press in 1979, was written by James Botkin, Mahdi Elmandjra, and Mircea Malitza. These men describe an understanding consistent with that being used in this book:

> For us, learning means an approach, both to knowledge and to life, that emphasizes human initiative. It encompasses the acquisition and practice of new methodologies, new skills, new attitudes, and new values necessary to live in a world of change. Learning is the process of preparing to deal with new situations. It may occur consciously, or often unconsciously, usually from experiencing real-life situations, although simulated or imagined situations can also induce learning. Practically every individual in the world, whether schooled

or not, experiences the process of learning—and probably none of us at present are learning at the levels, intensities, and speeds needed to cope with the complexities of modern life.

In that same report, "maintenance learning" is described as that which is available to most people around the world. Maintenance learning operates out of what is already known. It often happens in hierarchical patterns. One result of maintenance learning is the continued control by those in whose hands power now lies. With maintenance learning, we are not likely to make many changes in the ways we live and learn.

In the United States, powerful forces are at work to convince people that only maintenance learning is necessary. Religious groups have joined forces with government and industry to impose on the rest of the public their convictions that education and society should remain the way they have been. Particularly through the mass media, messages come that would have us as Christians work to keep the world as it is.

Such messages deny the reality that the world has indeed already changed. Imogene Jackson's world of the early twentieth century, described in Chapter Two, is just not there any more. The people delivering the "no-change" messages seem to deny that any of the shifts described in Chapter Two have occurred. They refuse to accept the truth that God created all the world and all the people. They want only to continue what has been. New possibilities are not to be sought. Many of these appeals are cast in terms that appeal to religious people.

Given the situation in the world, maintenance learning is not adequate—neither in the congregation and its households nor in the society and its educating structures. More appropriate to the vision of Christians is what is called in the report "innovative learning."

The two qualities of innovative learning are anticipation and participation. Anticipation is the ability to deal with the future, to foresee coming events as well as to evaluate the consequences of decisions and actions. Participation in both local and global settings requires cooperation, dialogue, communication, reciprocity and empathy. These qualities are similar to those described in the next chapter as characteristics of those who are "in but not of the world."

Some of the forces and conditions from which we learn are more destructive of these qualities and characteristics than they are contributive to them. Some diminish our ability to participate actively in our own lives. They lessen the probability of all people having the possibility of living fully human lives.

As Christians, those who are called to live so life can be full and abundant for all people on earth, we must join with others in working with those forces consistent with our values and against those which do not enhance or may destroy those values.

Let's look at some of the educating forces listed on pages 53-54 and consider some of the ways in which the forces influence us. Some ways will be considered as to how the people of our congregations and households might work with others to influence the education that flows forth from some of the forces.

Schools, Colleges and Universities

People in one congregation worked actively to elect a member of the congregation to the school board. He served for six years, quite often being in the minority that wanted the education in the district to be more than maintenance learning. A woman with a similar viewpoint, who was elected to the school board, transferred her church membership to the congregation because of the support given to work in public education.

She had been a member of the school board for six years and decided not to run again. One of her responsibilities in the congregation was to help plan for speakers for the adult forum class. So she arranged for the eight candidates running for the school board to meet with the adult group one Sunday morning. Seven of the eight candidates responded to her invitation.

Each of the candidates gave a three-minute talk. Then there were questions. A school bond issue had been defeated in the community earlier in the year in spite of the work of the people in the congregation in favor of it. The question of financing the school system was a serious one.

One member of the congregation asked each of the candidates to state his or her priorities relative to programs, since it was obvious that small savings around the edges would not solve the financial problem.

The answers given and the inability or refusal to answer the question gave the large group gathered a good indication of the position of each candidate. After the session, one of the candidates remarked that the gathering had been the largest at which they had made presentations.

Church people could be among the concerned core of people working actively in relationship to the schools. In addition to supporting qualified candidates and study/action like that in the ·congregation, people from several congregations might come together to work on the issues of the area served by a particular school or by those of a whole school district. Cooperative efforts related to public education can be done through church-related agencies that work across district boundaries.

Through the initiative of some pastors, the council of churches serving an area including several cities as well as incorporated country areas held a half-day session centering on support for public education in the 80s. More than one hundred people attended the meeting, including school board members, administrative personnel, school principals, teachers, people from student services, pastors, lay church members, college personnel, representatives from United Ministries in Higher Education, people from PTA groups and a teachers' union executive. The participants came from nine school districts.

Twenty-five people indicated interest in working in ongoing support groups. A committee including some of that twenty-five worked through the council of churches. They provided a litany, a hymn and other resources to be used on a "Public Education Sabbath" during American Education Week.

Public schools in the United States are mirrors of the social ills currently among us: segregation in housing and employment . . . personal confusion about moral life . . . excessive mobility . . . instability in family life . . . lack of clarity about appropriate roles for women and men . . . resistance to the freeing of people from bondage due to race, sex, national origin, sexual orientation, physical handicaps, age . . . inflation and economic conflict . . . violence throughout life.

Our schools are the responsibility of us all. Christians can work to create and maintain quality schools and to insure that the right and opportunity to prepare for a fulfilling life are provided for every child and youth. The United States is among the countries in the world which have attempted to provide education for all people. It has been a noble experiment which will fail if well-meaning people allow it to do so.

Church members must accept responsibility for influencing changes in the life and conduct of schools and for providing other learning experiences for people. Many children receive little or no encouragement outside the classroom to use the skills they are learning. Church people can share with school leaders and others in the community the concern for renewal of educational provisions for each new generation.

In addition to study/action groups, other ways of supporting education are to make the building available for elections, tutoring sessions, English language classes for refugees, monitoring of school board meetings with reports back to the church members for action and ongoing support groups for professionals working in education.

Traditionally, the involvement of the church with higher education has been in providing church-related colleges and universities as well as campus ministry at tax-supported institutions of higher education. With the development of community colleges, the increase in commuter students, and the number of students beyond their mid-twenties continuing their education, some new models of ministry in higher education are coming into being.

Many congregations are now able and willing to be centers for such ministries rather than expecting that a minister on the campus would do such work on their behalf. In some places, most response is given to inquiries from congregations by the community relations office, which is concerned about such involvements by the college.

In one area, an interdenominational campus ministry was developed when two ministers gathered people from several congregations who decided to begin an area campus ministry. They hired one staff who carries out the ministry, develops and maintains links with 130 churches and nine colleges—seven of which are community colleges. Six denominations provide funding. The office for the staff is in one of the church buildings rather than on a campus in order to symbolize the primary role which congregations have in the ministry.

The new pastor of a church was hired because of his interest in working with the community college in town. Through recent years, the college and the congregation had worked together. People from the congregation were involved in the development of the college.

The college sought and was granted funding for a senior citizens' center. The college group turned to the congregation for space and facilities. The college provides seminars and courses for church school teachers and encourages the pastor to teach religion and philosophy courses.

Libraries, Museums, Voluntary Associations

Institutions like these are constantly in need of volunteers to carry out their educational tasks. One of the contributions which a congregation might be able to make in this area would be to consider that work with libraries, museums, and groups like Camp Fire, Boy Scouts, 4-H and the host of other community agencies is one way in which its members witness to their faith. Such groups provide avenues through which ministering to human hurt can happen. Often the church sees these groups as in competition with them for the time of the people of the congregation. A more creative response might be to encourage such activity by its members. Ways might be provided within the congregation to motivate people to continue to do such work.

The Mass Media

The people in the lifestyle assessment group had been meeting every week for twelve weeks. Then they took a vacation from that group while some of them participated in the Television Awareness Training sessions being held in the congregation.

When they began meeting again for the next twelve-week period, those who had experienced the awareness training were eager to share their new-found insights with the rest of the group. They also wanted to continue to experiment with being in control of television rather than being its victim. They knew the chances of continuing to do that were more likely if they had the support of the group.

As they had done during the training, they listed their own viewing, analyzed the content of programs and advertising seen and decided to limit the number of hours of viewing each week. They set up a bulletin board in their meeting space on which they posted their "report cards" each week. A part of their agenda weekly was to talk about what was happening to them and their families in the process.

The only ones from the group who had attended the Television Awareness Training session were those with children still at home. The couples without children at home and the single-member families who were in the lifestyle group found value in being able to control their involvement with television. All agreed that it was helpful to talk about what was happening to them and what and how they were learning.

Consider Television Awareness Training as a way of helping people in the congregation cope with television as a positive influence instead of a monster in the house. It is designed to help people evaluate what happens when they view television. It is focused on the role of the viewer, not the broadcaster or the sponsor, in upgrading the quality of what television brings into homes. Television Awareness Training is a nonsectarian, non-profit cooperative project designed by United Methodist Communications, American Lutheran Church, Church of the Brethren, and Media Action Research Council, Inc. (For more information, write to Media Action Research Center, 475 Riverside Drive, Suite 1370, New York City, New York, 10015.)

The Military

As in the case with many of the educating forces in our society, the military is directly involved with education of those within its structures. Of more importance to the work of the congregations and their households is the military mindset prevalent in our world that undergirds and supports military activity.

For many people, that military mindset is in conflict with the vision or dream appropriate to Christians. The military mindset reinforces negative, destructive qualities among us. The military mindset limits both participation and anticipation which are the qualities of innovative learning identified above as consistent with the Christian gospel.

Participation and anticipation are limited by hierarchical decision-making, by competition, by national interest, and by the use of resources for war and preparation for war. As Christians, we are called to participatory decision-making, cooperation, global responsibility, and the use of resources for constructive purposes.

It is not so much that the military mindset has created the negative dimensions but rather that it is a manifestation of those conditions among us. The combination of all of these in the military mindset and the pervasiveness of that among us are what is dangerous. More fundamental as an issue against which Christians must witness is the attitude that would have us consider some of the people of the world as enemies and therefore expendable. Taking on ourselves as human beings the right of life and death over others is one illustration of our human inclination to act as gods.

The constant reinforcement of a "national security" perspective through the media and the actions of government and military people is an illustration of the military mindset. Fear of other people is engendered and enhanced by such attitudes.

In *No Limits To Learning,* it is reported that "almost half of the world's scientists are engaged in 'defense' projects, and . . . military expenditure now exceeds one billion dollars a day . . . . In 1976, the world spent 60 times as much money to equip each soldier as it spent educating each child."

Many forces in our society work to encourage competitive attitudes in men and passive responses among women. Many women in recent years have begun to train themselves to be more assertive. Perhaps men need to participate in training to be more cooperative in sessions similar to those called assertiveness training events. Evidence of the drive toward competition and rivalry can be seen in the widespread involvement with sports which require some people to be losers.

In many of our schools, we teach world relations, world history, American history and American government as though the United States were the center of the universe and wars were significant landmarks of history. Social, intellectual and economic history are often neglected in favor of political and military history.

Within the activities and attitudes of the church it might be possible to stess the positive values of the gospel and counter the military mindset.

The Whole Congregation Teaches

The church is an educating force in our communities along with the other groups listed earlier in this chapter. With its Sunday morning church school, the congregation provides the community with opportunities for people of all ages to learn. Through its other educational offerings, many possibilities for learning are available.

In this section, however, we will look at the church as an educating influence from a different angle. We will consider how education in the faith happens in the midst of the whole life of the congregation. To this point in the chapter, we have been looking at the community and the forces that educate people both in and out of the church. Let us apply that same kind of analysis to the life within the congregation.

C. Ellis Nelson in *Where Faith Begins* states: "Faith is communicated by a community of believers. The meaning of faith is developed by its members out of their history, by their interaction with each other, and in relation to the events that take place in their lives." Roger Shinn in *The Educational Mission of Our Church* makes a similar statement: "We need to remove from our minds the notion that the Christian faith is directly dependent upon any instructional agencies or methods and fix in our minds the idea that faith is fostered by a community of believers, usually a congregation."

Think about the story of John (told at the beginning of this chapter), and consider the kinds of questions and issues that must have been raised for the people when he began to show up in their midst again. Consider what must have happened in some of the times when John was with them which enabled him to know about and depend on their love.

In those encounters with each other, John and the other people in the congregation were both teaching and learning all the time. What do people learn in your congregation apart from the scheduled learning times? What activities or attitudes in your congregation are likely to encourage people to return? What might you be doing that would help people decide not to come back?

A young man who is now a pastor tells why he continued to come to a congregation as a child and youth. His parents were not involved in the church at all. They came from two rather diverse religious heritages and decided to send him to the nearest Protestant church for his religious training.

He was in third grade when he began attending church school. At that time, the congregation was using curriculum materials for church school that included a message to parents each quarter. Usually that message to parents was mailed. At least once each year, the church school teachers were expected to deliver the pamphlet in person. Several attempts were made to call in his home but the teacher never got past the narrow opening of the door through which the message was slipped into the hand of one of his parents.

The young man talks of people calling him by name and making him feel like a significant human being. He remembers a junior high school teacher who would come by the grocery store where he worked to give him information about activities.

One of the ways that John experienced the care of the people of the congregation was through the credit union. It was a factor in his journey back into the church. What programs and ministries in your congregation might be similar ones with which a person might make an initial contact without coming to either church school or worship?

In one congregation, people were attracted to some of the church's activities because the building was available for use by community groups important to them. A church in a very small town decided they should let their building be open so their toilets would be available for public use. It meant extra work was necessary but it was a needed service in that town. Through such ministries, people learn about us in ways often unknown to us.

Anything that happens in a congregation and its households has the possibility of being a basis for learning for someone. People learn concepts, values, principles of the faith that are evident through such vehicles for learning as . . .

   . . . how the telephone is answered,

   . . . how they are greeted and by whom,

   . . . which rooms are assigned to which groups,

   . . . allocations of funds in the church and household budgets,

   . . . how decisions are made in both the household and the congregation,

   . . . what kind of sharing is done,

. . . which community groups use the building,
. . . what the buildings and rooms smell and look like,
. . . what is on the bulletin boards and walls,
. . . what magazines are available to read,
. . . music sung and heard,
. . . who does which jobs,
. . . the style of the service of worship,
. . . and so on—through all the dimensions of life in the congregation and the household.

The congregation involves people of all ages. It is a ready-made setting for demonstrating the need for lifelong learning as well as for helping us be aware of the ways in which learning needs and responses are different at different times of our lives. We know that because we see people of all ages learning many things in many ways.

We really do not know how or when or where people learn. But when we observe transformed, changed, growing people, we know that learning has happened.

II.
People of Our Congregations and Households

CHAPTER FIVE

The Joyous Tensions of Servanthood

An Overview

The image of the church described in Chapter One was that it is a community of Christians of faith, hope, and love. In this chapter, those who live in, but not of, the world are identified as those who can live in a balance between the tensions, the paradoxes into which life thrusts us. Qualities of people of faith, hope, love and joy are described.

The story of Carolyn and Roger tells what can happen when a family decides to spend their energies in working to help others to healthier, fuller lives. Their lives are a demonstration of being people of faith, hope, love and joy.

The dream, the vision for the world out of which Roger and Carolyn live is implicit in their story. All of us dream or have visions that illuminate our lives. In this section, false dreams that can lead us astray, world-changing dreams and those appropriate to the vision of the gospel are discussed.

In But Not Of the World

Jesus was concerned about the outcasts of society but did not join them. Rather, he lifted up possibilities for their creative living within the limitations placed on them. At the same time Jesus confronted those of the system of his day with the inadequacy of their responses to life. He was in but not of that world. His values were obviously different from those of others.

Followers of Jesus are called to be servants. That does not mean picking up after other people. What is required is the decision to adapt ourselves no longer to the pattern of this culture in which we live. That is a crucial decision that provides the possibility of living as a Christian, as a servant.

In Chapter One, the church was described as a community of Christians of faith, hope and love. In this chapter, we will use those same categories and add that of joy to our description of those who live in but not of the world—those who are not conformed to this world but are transformed ones.

Faith

Those who live in but not of the world know that life is paradoxical. Life seems to contradict itself. We are called to live in the tension between seemingly opposite realities. Authentic faith is expressed in the deliberate placing of oneself in the tensions between revelation and reason, trust and doubt, affirmation and analysis, secular and sacred. It is the decision to live within the tensions of law and gospel, between obligation and freedom.

The witness of the scripture and of people of faith through the years is that inauthentic faith is that which rejects the tensions. Inauthentic faith is not a wrong statement of belief or doctrine. It is making a too-easy compromise with one side of the paradoxes of faith. For both the sacred and the secular are present in all of life. The person of total trust is not faithful but naive. The one who doubts everything is a cynic. The person of law or obligation is guilty of narrow legalism while the one of absolute freedom is licentious.

We identify a person of faith not as the one with correct ideas but as the one who experiences wonder at the tragic and beautiful mystery encountered in the ambiguous tension that everyday life actually is.

Hope

What happens to people who decide to live such a life is amazing. Life is transformed. The awareness that there is something-other-than-human which controls our life, setting limits within which our human activity must take place, which sustains and nurtures life within those limits—such an awareness brings with it the experience of freedom.

Life as it is given to us is a divine gift. We can live out the possibilities present within our limited human sphere. Creativity bubbles up out of the deeps of our being. That is what hope is about for Christians. Hope has to do with a present reality, a dimension of life here and now, for that is all we have. It is freely choosing to live in the paradoxical tension of life as it actually is. We live between life and death, victory and defeat, past and future.

Inauthentic hope is not misplaced loyalty or false expectations of a dreamed-of future, but is the refusal to hold the paradoxes in tension. The person who denies death is a romantic. The one who denies the value of life is bent toward self-destruction. The one who claims there is no defeat in life lives in illusions while one who can never admit victory creates the self-fulfilling prophecy of never-ending defeat. The person who lives only in the past is already dead. The one who lives only in the future is a visionary dreamer whose dreams are never fulfilled. The person of hope today is one who is self-consciously aware of the present moment as a gift.

Love

The statement that life is given as a gift carries with it an imperative. In the words of the old hymn: "Because I have been given much, I, too, must give." In some strange way, with the awareness of freedom comes the urge to serve. This is not an imposed rule but is just a description of what happens. For Christians, love is a relationship rather than an attitude.

We are called to love God and our neighbor as they confront us in Jesus Christ. We are always in that tension when we are faithful. The right relationship with God must be combined with our being servants in the world. Love is evident in the tension between charity and justice, individual and society, action and reflection.

Inauthentic love is not a wrong feeling toward one's neighbor but the too-easy compromise with one side of those tensions. The charitable person often demeans those who receive charity. The one concerned only about justice is often blind to suffering. The individualist denies the social structures necessary for justice, while the mob destroys liberty. Action without reflection is often misguided and reflection with no action is empty. The person who loves today is the comprehensively responsible one who expends life in the midst of contradictory covenants. The question never is whether to love, but who and how to love.

Joy

Those who decide to live their lives in the tensions of these paradoxes are also those who experience authentic joy. Joy appears in the midst of living in faith as intentional ones in ambiguous tension, in hope as people aware of the present moment as a gift from God and in love as comprehensive ones in the midst of contradictory covenants. There is a sense of fulfillment and peace about these people who live in but not of the world. It is a tranquillity like that of the calm sea, that in the eye of a tornado, that in the center of a whirlwind, in a state that those who live of the world may think is crazy.

Joy is present in the tension between pain and pleasure, comedy and tragedy, involvement and indifference. Inauthentic joy is not the inability to smile but the refusal to hold these paradoxes in tensions. For the one who only sees comedy in life is simpleminded. The one for whom all of life is tragic is a fatalist. The one involved in everything is eaten up by the details of life. The completely indifferent one is callous and selfish. The person of joy today is the passionately engaged one who experiences the peace which passes understanding.

These ideas about people who live in but not of the world are simply descriptive of the way life is. They are not a prescription about how life ought to be. They are not formulas to follow but are just the way it is in life. Such people are the ones of whom Isaiah wrote:

Those who wait on the Lord shall renew their strength.
They shall mount up on wings as eagles.
They shall run and not be weary.
They shall walk and not faint.

An Illustration of Responsible Servants

Carolyn and Roger met when they were students in college. She majored in home economics and he in philosophy and religion. Just before they were married, the offer came to them to go to Nigeria as teachers. Roger could serve in that way as an alternative to service in the military.

For three years they were teachers of history, geography, English, religious knowledge and domestic science. Scarcely older than their students, they identified easily with the Nigerian youth, working with them in the classroom, in clubs, in sports, in their home and at church.

In a March 1970 letter, they told their friends that they had decided against a second tour in Nigeria. They were instead going to settle in Minnesota and work with Roger's family on the farm. They did that.

Just over a year later, they were asked to return to Nigeria so Roger could be the business manager and treasurer of the Garkida and Lassa hospitals. He and Carolyn had Nigerian entry visas which were difficult to get at that time. After much prayer and thought, they decided to disengage themselves from the house and farm in Minnesota and go back to Nigeria.

This time, they stayed for five years. During that time, their two sons were born. Roger worked as coordinator of medical services. Carolyn did some teaching but was mostly involved with the care of the family.

The hospitals and medical programs with which Roger worked had been initiated nearly fifty years before by missionaries from the United States. The health system covered 10,000 square miles and served 800,000 people. He coordinated the work of three general hospitals, a leprosy hospital, eight dispensaries, three maternity units, six mobile teams and helped to establish a village-based health program for 90 villages.

A major part of his job from 1971-76 was to work himself and the other ex-patriate workers out of their jobs. In an interview in 1974, he talked of the satisfaction that came in sharing the hopes and joys of the people with whom he worked. Seeing the Nigerians accept responsibilities was particularly rewarding. He said, "They can get things done that we as foreigners could never do. They understand the people and their needs. They know how to deal with red tape. There is no question that they can handle the medical program."

Roger has told the story of the decision of a black Christian congregation in Nigeria to send missionaries to North America and Europe. He said, "It came as a surprise to some people who support white missionaries serving in Africa. Actually, these Nigerians wanted to share their belief in living a simple life and to advocate extension of human rights in white countries. Any country where there is no need for orphanages and there isn't such a thing as an old people's home has a lot to be said for it."

In their 1975 Christmas letter, they described the shifts being made to government responsibility for the hospitals, writing, "We anticipate that our job here in Nigeria will be finished next year. We don't know where we'll be headed. We pray for an openness and willingness to accept the next challenge God has for our family. We are thankful for the growth we have experienced in the eight years here in Nigeria and hope that we will be able to use our increasing maturity wherever we are to help others see the glory and love of God."

In 1976, they returned again to the family farm in Minnesota. Not long after their arrival, they received and accepted the call to be pastors of a congregation of about 120 members. The church was located not far from the farm. When Carolyn was asked about the family's ability to live on a pastor's small salary, she replied, "We'll have a garden—a big one. We'll be raising chickens and rabbits to help out with the grocery bill."

During the summer of 1978, Roger responded to a request from the Presbyterian Church of Cameroun. He surveyed the primary health care needs of that country on their behalf.

In 1979, the Sudan Council of Churches decided to develop a primary health care system for the people of the Upper Nile Province of Sudan. Because they knew of the similar work done by the Church of the Brethren in Nigeria, they asked the Brethren to provide personnel to help them initiate the system. Roger was asked to be field coordinator of the new project.

Words from their 1979 Christmas letter hint at the difficulty of making the decision to go to Sudan: "We have been richly blessed this past few months in so many ways. We have experienced rich challenges and another rewarding year in our life in the Lewiston community. Each day we grow closer to the folk here and these contacts stretch our thoughts and broaden our understanding of God's family and our part in it.

"In spite of our joy in living with our friends here, our future holds another move. The Sudan Council of Churches has invited the Church of the Brethren to help in establishing a new primary health care program. We have said yes to the request and are now making the many preparations needed for that response. It was a difficult decision to make in light of our favorable situation here at Lewiston and the uncertainty of what a minimum of three years in that setting would mean in the development of Jon (8 years old) and Jedd (6 years old). But we have learned that all will work toward the glory of God if we trust his guidance. That gives us the courage to proceed."

After making the decision to go, Carolyn began to learn to play the recorder. She saw it as a source of relaxation for herself as well as a means of teaching the boys about music. She spent much time in selecting the appropriate educational materials for the teaching that she and Roger will do with the boys during the three years they expect to be in Sudan.

In an April 1980 report, they described their situation. They were working directly for the Sudan Council of Churches and would live under the same conditions as all other employees. They would be living in a new village about sixty miles away from the nearest town. The area is on the edge of what is the world's largest swamp, which makes overland transportation impossible for at least half of the year. The river system they had hoped to use had been blocked with water hyacinths for the nine months before their report.

In that same report, they said that the tasks for the first year would be establishing a home and preparing for the project. The preparation would include learning about local needs and resources, establishing relationships with government officials, preparing a program budget and schedule. They expect also to become proficient in the Nuer language, the dialect of the area in which they will live, as well as Arabic which is the language of the country. At the beginning of their second term in Nigeria, they had studied Hausa. They reported some frustration in trying to master a new language but said, "The joy and freedom of being able to communicate with the people even on an elementary level far outweighs the frustrations."

Their first worship experience in Nuerland was on Easter Sunday 1980. About seventy people gathered in the church which was Presbyterian in heritage. They met at eight in the morning before the heat of the day. All Christians of the area worshipped together—Presbyterian, Catholic, and now Brethren—in what is the only church in Wang Kai.

In response to Roger's question to a Catholic priest in Bentin about whether the Roman Catholic Church expected to build a church in Wang Kai, the priest said, "No. Since we all worship the same Christ we should join together in our celebrations and not compete."

The Easter service was conducted by an elder of the church. In the prayer, he called upon the Sudanese church to send them a pastor and gave thanks for the coming of Roger and Carolyn to help them. In the conversations following the service, none of the people asked for missionary evangelists. They hinted that they could provide that leadership themselves. But they are willing that foreigners with technical expertise come to help them learn to help themselves.

The sermon was based on John's acount of Jesus as the vine. Roger and Carolyn said that it seemed appropriate that with the hope of Easter, these Christians emphasized our responsibility to be faithful to the tasks to which we are called.

Of Dreams and Visions

It seems likely that Carolyn and Roger share a vision, a dream about the way the world can be that motivates them to say yes to invitations to serve and that sustains them in the midst of that work. They obviously live out of understandings about life that are different in some ways from those of many other people.

T. E. Lawrence wrote:

> All persons dream but not equally. They who dream by night in the dusty recesses of their minds wake up in the day to find that it's vanity . . . . But the dreamers of the day are dangerous humans for they act out their dreams with open eyes to make them possible.

Dreaming and visioning are part of everyday life. We do it all the time. The universality of dreaming can be seen in words of music in recent years. "You've got to have a dream. If you don't have a dream, how're you going to have a dream come true?" A song which speaks of the same quality as Lawrence's dangerous dreamers is from "The Man of LaMancha." It says, "to dream the impossible dream, to right the unrightable wrong . . . ."

Self-conscious dreaming — the dreaming of the day — has been called by a variety of names. Some call such dreams visions. Others call them long-range planning. For some, prayer could be the label put on this kind of activity of dangerous humans. The kind of passionate intentionality in the statement that "prayer is the soul's sincere desire" is present in self-conscious dreaming.

When we dream and create visions, we are trying to express the nearly inexpressible. We use poetry and symbols, dreams and visions, song, parables and stories in the teaching ministry of the church to express that which cannot be said easily.

Given this kind of universality of dreaming, it is not surprising that the scripture contains many references to dreams, dreamers, visions and prophets. Ezekiel, Daniel, Isaiah, the Josephs of both the Old and New Testaments, Mary, Herod and John on Patmos are only a few of the biblical dreamers.

Dreams and visions can provide motivation for beginning and continuing the tasks to be done. They can be a basis for planning what to do next and evaluating what has happened before. Abram's vision was what sustained him as he moved his people away from their home into a foreign land. The Joseph of the Old Testament was both a dreamer and an interpreter of dreams. He learned in his later years to share his dreams so that sharing was not as destructive as that of his youth. He learned how to use his dreams as a way of helping a country to move in a different way.

False Dreams

A song from the musical "Joseph and the Amazing Technicolor Dreamcoat" says:

> I closed my eyes, drew back the curtain
> To see for certain what I thought I knew.
> Far, far away, someone was weeping,
> But the world was sleeping. Any dream will do . . .
> The light is dimming and the dream is, too.
> The world and I, we are still waiting,
> Still hesitating. Any dream will do.

That is not true. It is not true that any dream will do. Listen to some of the warnings from scripture:

> Ask of the Lord rain in the autumn,
>   ask for rain in the spring,
> The Lord who makes the storm-clouds,
>   will give you showers of rain and
>   grass in your field;
> for the household gods make mischievous promises;
> diviners see false signs,
> they tell lying dreams and talk raving nonsense.
> The people wander about like sheep
>   in distress for lack of a shepherd.
>   Zechariah 10:1-2

> Do not listen to what the prophets say,
>   who buoy you up with false hopes;
> the vision they report springs from their own imagination,
>   it is not from the mouth of the Lord.
>   Jeremiah 23:16

So how can we know when the dreams are false and futile? How can we know which to spend our energy and lives on? What kinds of dreams are raving nonsense?

Dreams and visions — regardless of who is sharing them — are illusory nonsense when they allow us to escape from our real-life situations. They are false when they lead us to refuse to accept reality as it is given to us. This can happen in several ways.

One kind of false dreams are those which say: "If only . . . then . . . " People in the church say to each other: "If only we had more money, more people, more . . . , then we would be a great church." or, "If only we had different church school materials, another pastor, different . . . , then we would do great things." In our households, we think and sometimes say: "If only I had married a different person, then . . . " or, "If only we had a bigger house, a different job, more grateful children, . . . then we would be a great family."

Those are false dreams because the money you have, the people you are with, the church and the world as they are, the family you have are gifts not problems. This is not to say that the way things are is the way they ought to be or have to stay. But certainly what you presently have on your hands is what you must start with, the situation out of which change might develop.

Another way in which we try to escape from reality in our dreams and visions is to deal with either the past or the future without taking the present seriously. Some false dreams deal only with the past or only with the future. Those words from Joel that Peter used in his Pentecost speech speak of the young seeing visions and the old dreaming dreams. (Joel 2:28, Acts 2:17). Those are not false dreams if they deal with the present and identify action in which to engage.

A young man shared his vision with a group of what the church might be. He talked of what the ministry of education might include in the future. His dream was vivid and intriguing. In response to questions about what needed to be done that his dream might become reality, he could not describe any way that he needed to be involved in doing that. He was not ready to take any responsibility in the present for seeing that the vision might become reality. His vision was set off in some dreamy future with no connection with his present action.

My father was nearly ninety years old when I last visited him. He was clear about what was happening around him most of the time. His conversation, though, was about the glories of the past. He yearned for yesterdays long gone. His dreaming was only of the past.

The experience of the past will become part of our dreams and visions as will our consideration of possible futures. Our dreams and visions must also be that which enables us to live in the present as it is given to us. Our educational structures and nurturing in congregations and households must be that which helps people to maintain their connection with the past and anticipate the future while participating creatively in the present.

Another way in which dreams are false is when they are reduced in time and space or concept from what is required of us by the gospel. If our dreams are only for ourselves, or only for our household, or only for our congregation, or only for our denomination, or only for people like us, they are misleading visions. The dreams and visions to which the gospel calls us are for the whole of God's created earth and for all the people of the world.

Dreams may turn out to be empty and powerless if they are shared in a way that the people to whom they are told cannot comprehend them. Young Joseph's style of telling his dreams is an example of how that can happen. His dream-sharing puzzled his father and angered his brothers.

Dreams are more likely to become reality if they are shared by others. To quote Dom Helder Camara, "When we dream alone, it remains only a dream. When we dream together, it is not just a dream, it is the beginning of reality."

World-changing dreams

World-changing dreams have four characteristics. They are universal and particular, global and comprehensive, future-oriented and that which requires commitment of us.

1. World-changing dreams are universal at the same time they are particular. The world was changed when the large dream of sailing around the world became reality. That happened in the particular action of a group of people actually leaving port.

2. World-changing dreams are global and comprehensive. Karl Marx sat in a library in England and had a dream of how working-class people could take some control over their own destinies. His dream became a reality with world-changing consequences. Patterns of politics, economics and culture were radically altered all over the earth.

3. World-changing visions are future-oriented. They take into account the heritage of the past, consider the reality of the present, and paint realistic pictures of the possibilities for the future. An example of this is the space program. Ideas about what could be were developed far in advance of the first launches. A picture of the future was created years before the trip to the moon actually happened. That trip literally changed our image of the earth. We now know ourselves to be riding on a mysteriously beautiful bluish ball floating in black space. Our old dreams of nationalistic supremacy or local community self-sufficiency seem petty and unimportant in light of that new image of the earth.

4. World-changing dreams and visions require commitment. They demand a willingness to risk our lives, a willingness to give up individual preference for corporate action. Think, for instance, of how many people have been trained in the armed forces of this country through the years and how many people died in the wars of the last few decades. They died for a dream of spreading American democracy around the world—a vision that has become increasingly empty. But people were willing to risk and to lose their lives for such a dream.

The vision of the gospel

Some dreams and visions that have all those qualities are not appropriate for the Christian. Christians necessarily have another dimension that must be present in their dreams and visions.

We are called to be creators with God of a world in which each one can live "neath a vine and fig tree, at peace and unafraid." That message is stated several times in the Scripture. Among them are Matthew 25 and Luke 4. Another such statement is in Isaiah 58:

Is not this what I require as a fast:
   to loose the fetters of injustice,
   to untie the knots of the yoke,
     to snap every yoke
     and set free those who have been crushed:
Is it not sharing your food with the hungry,
   taking the homeless poor into your house,
   clothing the naked when you meet them
   and never evading a duty to your kinsfolk?
Then shall your light break forth like the dawn . . .
Then, if you call, the Lord will answer;
   if you cry to him, he will say, "Here I am."
   if you cease to pervert justice,
   to point the accusing finger and lay false charges,
   if you feed the hungry from your own plenty
     and satisfy the needs of the wretched,
   then your light will rise like dawn out of darkness
     and your dusk will be like noonday . . . ;
you shall be called rebuilder of broken walls,
   restorer of houses in ruins.

Isaiah here is raising the unavoidable demands of social justice, of sympathy and compassion, of love of neighbor and renewed self-identification with God. These same demands were stated by Jesus in the synagogue at Nazareth.

The particulars of the situations were different in the times of the prophet and of Jesus than they are now. But pain, suffering, injustice and human need are still realities among us. Our experiencing of the presence of God with us still happens when we participate with others in bringing relief to the hungry and justice to the oppressed.

That vision of what life could be when God's realm is recognized on earth is that which Jesus as Messiah came to proclaim, to witness to and to die for. It is that vision we are called upon to live. That is the context for our world-changing dreams. To become reality, our dreams and visions must have the qualities of any world-changing dreams but also have the added dimension which the Christian context provides.

1. World-changing dreams of the Christian are universal and particular. A universal understanding is that the God we serve is a continuing creator of all the universe who loves all the people of the earth equally. Jesus as the Christ was an example of that universal love. He met particular human needs in specific situations.

We too are called to demonstrate that universal love as we relate to specific people in particular circumstances. This may mean that we decide to change our ways of living. Being in the small proportion of the world's population which controls most of the world's goods, we might decide that a demonstration of love would be to work with others on particular actions that would lead to more equitable distribution of those goods.

2. World-changing dreams of the Christian are global and comprehensive. Whatever actions we take in local situations are reflections of the world's problems. As we create structures that will provide food to the hungry in our neighborhoods, we are dealing with what is a global problem. The plans we make must be those which deal with as many dimensions of a problem as possible. For instance, it is not enough that we consider only what needs to happen in the political arena of life, we must also take into account the social and economic dimensions as well.

3. World-changing dreams of the Christian are future-oriented. Rubem Alves, a theologian from South America, has said that we must quit planting pumpkin seeds in order to have pie next season and begin planting dates in order that our children's children may have food.

4. World-changing dreams of the Christian are those which require from us. We are called to give our whole lives, to risk our deaths, to expend our energies while alive to bring to reality our dreams.

Your dream may be different from mine. It probably is. Your criteria for visions may be different from mine. But each of us operates out of our own dreams and those of others.

One of the most famous dream speeches of recent times is that of Martin Luther King, Jr., in August of 1963. Thousands have heard it. Hundreds have worked to bring that dream to reality since then and continue to do so.

King was willing to die for that dream. He did not just risk his physical death but was able to pour out his life energies to bring that vision to reality. Inscribed on the plaque in Memphis where King was shot are the words from Genesis that his brothers said about Joseph: "Here comes the dreamer. Come now, let us kill him and we shall see what becomes of his dreams."

CHAPTER SIX

Everyone is Special

An Overview

A description of a picture directory of one congregation is provided as an illustration of the varieties of households which are discussed in the first part of the chapter.

The next section of the chapter deals with the varieties of people who are part of our households and congregations at any one time and through time. Descriptions of people of different ages are given as a tiny window through which to glimpse that variety and to be an illustration of what might be expected to be happening to some of the people who are the ages of those described. Ways of teaching people of various ages are considered in Chapter Nine.

Some ideas about grouping people for learning are then offered along with an example of how one congregation successfully did it.

It may be an unusual congregation. The people in the congregation had not thought much about the kinds of families, the varieties of households that were part of it. Then they printed a picture directory. The photographs presented an interesting "picture" of the congregation.

About one-fourth of the pictures were of only one person. Several of these people had never married. Some were formerly married—widowed, divorced, separated. Some were parents, some grandparents, a few great-grandparents. The range in age of both those never married and those formerly married was from early twenties to two over ninety years old.

Another one-third of the pictures showed a man and a woman with one or more children. Four of these included his children and her children. In one, his two and her three were shown with their two. One example of this kind of family was the husband with his three sons and the wife with her son and daughter. His daughter lived with his former wife. When one of his sons was baptized into the church when he was in the seventh grade, all eight of these people gathered at the side of the baptismal pool.

One picture was of two men, three women and a dog. These single people were all volunteers working for the church. They lived in a five-bedroom house, sharing meals and household chores as well as an attachment to the dog who had lived through several generations of volunteers.

Several of the pictures were of women with one or more children. Some of these women were widows. Many of them were divorced or separated. Only two pictures were of a man with children.

In three of the pictures, three generations were shown. The wife's mother, the wife's father and the husband's mother were shown in pictures with the couples and from one to four children.

Varieties of Households

One assumption out of which planners in many congregations operate is that the households of the congregation include mostly families with a wage-earning father, a home-making mother and children. According to a January 20, 1980, article in the *Chicago Tribune* by Carol Kleiman, only 13 percent of American households are like that. In 21 percent of the households, both parents are working. Nearly one-third, 30 percent, are childless couples or those with no children at home. Single parents with children live in eight percent of the households. Adults live alone in 21 percent of them. The other seven percent report a variety of living arrangements, including three-generation households.

The word HOUSEHOLD is used in this book instead of the word FAMILY because it gives us the possibility of having images of the family in addition to the traditional one. A household includes one or more people who live in one or more rooms identifiably separate from other households. Households can be both decisional and natural. In what used to be considered a normal family, husband and wife were decisionally related to each other and naturally related to their children.

Use of the word household is consistent with Paul's declaration in Ephesians 2:19 that we are no longer aliens in a foreign land but are members of the "household of God." The households in which we live become households of faith when the members live in such a way that they know themselves to be members of that world-wide household of God.

Households and individuals may have been self-sufficient at some time in human history. Even if that were true at some other time and place, it is not true now. It is inconsistent with our faith to think that we are independent. Knowing that mutual interdependence is dynamic rather than static, we can help people deal with the nature of their covenant with God and their covenants with each other. Our congregational ministries should be those which help people in the households of the congregation to develop and maintain their commitments—to be people of integrity with relationships of trust and mutual interdependence.

In order to provide a realistic basis for planning for the congregation's ministries, consider doing a survey to identify the kinds of households in the congregation and the ages of the people in them. The forms printed below were designed to help planners in the congregation to get a clearer picture of the congregation's households and people.

CONGREGATIONAL HOUSEHOLD INVENTORY								
FAMILY NAME List family name only if all members of the household share the same name. If they do not, list both personal and family names in the spaces provided.								
ADULTS LIVING IN THE HOUSEHOLD—For each adult listed, indicate marital status with letters; S-single; M-Married, D-divorced separated; W-widow/widower in the SEX column.								
NAME	SEX		AGE					
	F	M	under 25	25-39	40-54	55-69	70 and over	
OTHERS LIVING IN THE HOUSEHOLD								
NAME	SEX		AGE					
	F	M	under 5	5-8	9-12	13-16	17-22	over 22

The *Congregational Household Inventory* gives space for recording the people living in each household, listing name, age, sex and marital status. These 5½″ × 8½″ sheets are available in quantity from The Brethren Press, 1451 Dundee, Elgin, Illinois, 60120 for a nominal cost. With each order, an 8½″ × 11″ *Household Inventory Summary Sheet* is provided free.

HOUSEHOLD INVENTORY SUMMARY SHEET														
Adults										Children and Youth				
	MARITAL STATUS—SEX													
AGE	single		married		div. sep.		widowed		TOTALS	AGE	female	male	TOTALS	
	F	M	F	M	F	M	F	M						
Under 25										Under 5				
25–39										5–8				
40–54										9–12				
55–69										13-16				
70 and over										17–22				
22 and over														
TOTALS NOTES										TOTALS				

The summary sheet has space for recording the information from the other sheets. This information is then available so those who plan can provide ministries appropriate to the actual situation in the congregation.

Varieties of People

Not only are the households of the congregation different from each other, but the people who live in those households are a complex, delightful, frustrating collection of unique variations of the human being. As we grow and change, our understandings and abilities shift as does our witness. We continually change throughout our lifetimes. Our capacities for life and therefore our responses in faith change over time and accumulate through the years rather like the layers of an onion.

In *Will Our Children Have Faith?* John Westerhoff uses the words — experienced, affiliative, searching and mature faith — to describe four styles of faith through which people grow. EXPERIENCED faith is developed during early childhood. During later years of childhood, AFFILIATIVE faith develops. What he describes as SEARCHING faith is not developed before adolescence while MATURE faith is not developed before adulthood.

Westerhoff also uses the analogy of a tree to describe the mode of our growing:

First, a tree with one ring is as much a tree as a tree with four rings. A tree in its first year is a complete and whole tree, and a tree with three rings is not a better tree but only an expanded tree. . . . Second, a tree grows if the proper environment is provided, and if such an environment is lacking, the tree becomes arrested in its expansion until the proper environment exists. Each tree, however, does its own "growing" and has its own unique characteristics. . . . Third, a tree acquires one ring at a time in a slow and gradual manner. We do not see that expansion, although we do see the results, and surely we are aware that you cannot skip rings, moving from a one-ring to a three-ring tree. . . . Fourth, as a tree grows, it does not eliminate rings but adds each ring to the ones before, always maintaining all the previous rings as it expands.

(pp. 89-90)

The following descriptions of people of different ages have been created in the hope that they might provide pictures of what might be expected to be happening in people of their same ages. No suggestion is intended that what is described is "normal" behavior or experience. Each is just one possible example of literally a universe of possibilities.

TODD—2 years old

Todd has been brought to the church nursery since he was two weeks old. It is not a strange place to him. He is two years old now. The nursery room is brightly colored and gives him things on which to climb. The people there smile at him, talk with him, cuddle him if he wants that, and most of the time are his friends. Being separated from his parents is not always comfortable for him.

   Recently, Todd has begun to say "NO!" to his parents, to others his age in the nursery and to the adults who care for them in the nursery. Hearing others say no to him is beginning to help him understand limits for his own behavior. He and others in the nursery are able to play beside each other most of the time. Sometimes a flurry of disagreement happens when a needed toy is grabbed away from him or a favorite spot is already filled by someone else.

   Todd and other two-year-olds like to run. The fellowship hall with its open space is an invitation to the children to run in it. Perhaps it is more important for them to have that freedom of movement than for the ideas of "proper behavior" in church to be imposed on them. Todd picks up from others around him their attitudes toward him and toward other dimensions of life. Todd is not conscious of being a person of faith. His faith experiencing focuses on the important people in his world. He is being influenced, without his knowledge, by the examples, moods, actions, and language of the people of faith in his world.

SARAH—*5 years old*

Sarah sees life as a series of scenes, of experiences which are interesting and exciting but not much connected with each other, or so it seems to those who observe her. It is difficult for her to tell fact from fantasy. She likes to hear stories but enjoys them just as they are without much understanding about any moral precepts which might be added to them. Because her imagination is so vivid, sometimes she scares herself with feelings and understandings which are difficult for her to explain to someone else. When she wakes up at night afraid from a bad dream, being hugged and reassured that she is loved is very important.

Only occasionally does Sarah understand that there is another point of view than her own from which to look at the world. When another child is hurt, she can feel sympathy for the hurt when it is similar to something she has experienced.

Authority is experienced by Sarah through parents and parent-like figures. Uniforms, large physical size and even drivers of very large vehicles are symbols of authority for her. Sarah's world is mostly limited to her family and those she meets and knows from church and school. She does not separate people into categories by race or sex but is more likely to experience people as they are.

Sarah's thoughts and feelings are a mix of images and beliefs which have been given her consciously and unconsciously by the people she trusts and those which her own experience and creative imagination have provided her. Punishment and reward are generally the basis on which she makes decisions. The possible punishment and reward can be real or imagined to be influential in her decision-making.

The church community provides opportunities for her to play with others her own age as well as being with others of all ages. As she receives patience and love, Sarah is being given a base from which she can later in life talk about God.

MIKE—9 years old

    Mike is more interested in his friends at school and church than in anyone else. He has a secure base in the family from which to move into other relationships. He gives and receives love (though he certainly would not use that word to describe the experience) as he forms and maintains relationships with others near his age.

    He has been organizing the world into categories and concepts. Mike and his friends experiment with the world and are sorting out the 'real' from the 'unreal' on the basis of their experiences and conversations about those experiences. The outer world is becoming more orderly for Mike as his inner world of fantasy continues to develop. He can figure out how things happen and can work to make them happen again, given similar conditions. He sorts out relationships like cousins and grandparents not only for himself but also for his friends.

His thinking can be separated from his feelings. Stories and myths about people and happenings provide Mike with a sense of the flow of life. He identifies with real and portrayed heroes in history, present-day events and dramatic performances like those on the television. Because of his developing ability to see the world from another's perspective, play-acting and reenacting stories are ways in which he makes connections between the world now and the worlds of other times and places.

Although authority is sometimes questioned, it is usually done on the basis of Mike's own experience. When he has no basis for such questioning, he most often follows what his friends, his parents, his older brother and sister say and do.

Mike's ability to categorize allows him to classify people as well as things. Because of his strong need to belong, he feels a strong identification with "those like us." Activities, stories, conversations and experiences can provide the enlarging of "those like us" or a narrowing of it.

Because Mike understands cause and effect relationships now, he is able to make connections between action and pleasure or pain, and will often act out of that. Another dimension of decision-making for Mike is playing fair and getting even.

He experiences symbols and symbolic language as one-dimensional and literal. Images and symbols for God are likely to be personalized and anthropomorphic.

Mike enjoys doing things well and repeats those experiences at which he succeeds. He knows that he can do math well, and makes opportunities to demonstrate his ability. He is able to make sense out of the world by using simple categories as he works systematically to bring order out of chaos. Mike's involvement with the church centers around his friendships with others. His need to belong sometimes leads him to do things that his parents and other adults do not want him to do — like making and flying paper airplanes from the balcony after worship.

BECKY—13 years old

Both Becky's parents work away from home. She is a self-reliant person whose involvement in the church group has her in positions of leadership among the younger youth. She sings in the youth choir and is regular in attendance.

Becky is able part of the time to construct an image of herself as others see her. She is aware of the fact that others are doing the same. Her words and actions sometimes enhance the self-images of others — more often if they are girls her age than if they are boys. This mutual interchange allows Becky the possibility of taking a 'third-person' perspective on her relationships with other people, with things and happenings. This kind of interaction provides the base for self-identity and self-conscious value formation. Becky is very aware of the expectations of others. She checks with her friends about what they are wearing and doing as a basis for her own action. Sometimes she decides to do the opposite of what her friends do as a means of self-assertion.

She perceives that the 'others' in her world — both those actually in her world and those indirectly in it through music, television and stories — do not operate out of the same standards. Sometimes she is very much the obedient child of her parents. At other times, she is an assertive young woman operating out of her own understandings and those of her friends.

Becky is able to evaluate her own thinking and behavior but sometimes decides not to, preferring to depend on the values of others at times. Her beliefs, values and attitudes are beginning to move into not-yet-self-conscious patterns being much influenced by the values, beliefs and attitudes of others.

Authority is located for Becky in those who represent an accepted perspective — therefore, it shifts with the shifting of loyalties. Becky's identity and faith are derived from involvement with and loyalty to peer groups, family groups, social norms, expectations and stereotypes. She separates people into 'us' and 'them' with 'them' being understood in sometimes stereotypical and prejudicial terms.

Her decisions are made out of concern for maintaining peace among people and maintaining order among groups. Her religious talk about God centers on personal qualities such as friend, companion, guide, all-knowing, all-loving.

Becky and her friends like to deal with facts and accuracy. They like working with maps, outlines and timelines. She finds her individuality in the group of her friends. They sometimes talk nonsense and make rapid switches between 'silly kid stuff' and profound insights. They want to have many points of view presented as they are sorting out what might be 'right' for them.

JOE—17 years old

Joe's enthusiasm quite often runs faster than his experience can cope with. He and his best friend, Gary, spend many hours working at the intricacies of electronics while they create images of the future. They are both sure that what the world needs is for them to have a chance to organize it. They are ready for anything and think they can accomplish anything. Sometimes their focus on the future has them failing to do what is needed in the present.

Joe and Gary have great arguments in which at least two sides of almost any issue are found and stated. They can separate the world into 'right' and 'wrong' and argue from either viewpoint. They know themselves to have viewpoints which are their own and those which are different from those of others.

Joe's heroes are those who accomplish great things. Authenticity and consistency is expected between belief and action. Having the ability to interact with others in mutually helpful ways, Joe is very much involved with his age group at church. Those of the church school class are a primary nurture group for Joe. He eats with them at school, tries to get into the same classes and spends much time with them.

His language is often abstract. He struggles to get his ideas stated clearly and without ambiguity and quite often fails. With a perception of the viewpoints of others, Joe is very ready to defend his own point of view —even though that changes from time to time. In spite of such changes, a more and more self-conscious, consistent threat is beginning to emerge among his beliefs.

Authority for Joe must be consistent with his understanding of truth and his experience of reality. His decision-making is based on his strongly-held beliefs, but it has an unknown-to-him bias which comes out of his lack of experience beyond his own world.

Symbols and religious language and images have been translated into ideas and have lost some of the dimensions of magic and mystery. Joe struggles for explicit meanings, for internal consistency and for means of protecting the fragile boundaries of self and world understandings.

Joe appears to be his own greatest problem. He is an ethical puzzle to himself because he feels that his ideals are not manifest in his life. As he thinks for himself, he mistrusts the opinions of others if they do not check with his own perceptions. Quite often he hesitates to voice his own opinions when he thinks they may be counter to those of people considered to be authorities.

BOB *and* MARY—*two 24-year-olds*

Mary and Bob are both 24 years old. They were in high school at the same time. Both of their families have been involved in the congregation for many years.

Mary is now working at the bank as a cashier. She is not happy being classified by her church as one of the youth because she is not married. She knows herself to be a functioning responsible adult. She perceives that some of her friends have moved into what she calls 'traps' — one is in-

volved with a group which stops people at the airport to sell their literature; another has bought into the expectations of the culture with a home
in the suburbs and an all-absorbing family which seems to allow no outlet
for creativity; another is caught in the spiral of increasing demands of a
vocation in order 'to get ahead.'

She questions how the world is run. She sees and experiences
stupidity and self-seeking among her contacts in the world. Her relationships are good with those who work with her. Sometimes she feels a kind
of aimlessness in herself. Her close relationships include both men and
women. Mary is not convinced that marriage is necessary nor best for
everyone.

She is attending classes at the community college as she continues
her search for a vocation in life. Her study, work and social life provide
occasions in which she is applying her brain and exploring her feelings.
Her uncertainty about continuing to do the work at the bank for the rest
of her life is based on a concern for ethical principles like justice, human
equality and so on. Her involvement in church consists of regular attendance at the Sunday morning service of worship and sporadic participation in study groups and fellowship experiences as they are interesting
to her.

Bob, on the other hand, married young and is the father of two children. His participation in the congregation includes a willingness to share
in the education and care of the children. He shares some of the same
concerns about ethical principles that Mary does. An additional issue for
him is the parenting of his children and beyond that, the sharing of faith
with the younger generations of the congregation.

He is a teacher in a third grade classroom. Bob feels that teaching
provides him with opportunities to share his faith. His parents were able
to pay for his college education. This is his first year of working full-time.
He is finding it exciting and demanding. He and his wife share some of
their church and social activities. They plan their family life, however, so
that both participate actively in parenting and household work. They
schedule their participation so each is able to be involved with particular
special interests and concerns.

Bob's active involvement in the congregation is often experienced as
a member of his family more than as an individual. When he experiences
this assumption that he does not have an identity separate from his family
of origin and now his emerging family, Bob responds with patient ex-
planation and behavior that indicates his awareness of the need for individual integrity.

CATHY—53 years old

Cathy is a grandmother whose three children have all moved away from home, either married or in college. She is an executive for a social service agency. Her husband is the owner-manager of a successful publishing firm. Cathy finished her schooling during the early school years of the children and began working away from home when they were in junior high. Both she and her husband find their work very demanding.

At times, it seems like the job is eating her up.

In spite of the satisfaction of the job, she finds herself very tired at times. Fortunately, her recovery time is fairly short. Both she and her husband have developed ways of coping with their sense of uselessness in what they are doing.

In the midst of the monotony which goes with even exciting jobs, sometimes life sparkles and Cathy is joyous. When responding to demands on her through a sense of duty, an underlying wonder sometimes happens for her which transforms the everyday into something almost magical. Having come to terms with underlying ambiguities in her situation, Cathy experiences a multi-dimensional self-knowing that is both satisfying and frightening. Truth is seen as relative to the situation rather than an absolute removed from reality.

Cathy is critically aware of and transcends many of the cultural norms. Her experience with being a mother and a wife in other than the usual patterns enabled the development of that attitude. Having experienced suffering and loss, responsibility and failure, grief and joy, Cathy is able to experience and embrace the polarities which are present in life. Having developed a global perspective in which she can see the suffering of others, she feels forced to try to change her style of life from what it is to something more consistent with her values. She is becoming increasingly uncomfortable with her comfortable life.

Although she retains a sense of respect for authority, Cathy has come to depend on her own sense of what is appropriate for a given situation. 'Responsibility' is more likely to be her guide to appropriate behavior rather than an adherence to some abstract understanding of 'right' or 'good' response. She knows that what is right and what is good depends on the situation.

She has been able in recent years to reappropriate the Bible and the history of the church as her story and her community of identification. Biblical wisdom and stories are experienced as universal and hence hers. Myth and symbol have been rejoined with the ideas which reside in them. Cathy's strength comes from an inner experience of mystery which manifests itself in various ways. Her inclination toward meditation and contemplation is balanced by a strong drive toward action and involvement in life.

GEORGE— *75 years old*

George has been retired from his work as a carpenter for nearly five years. He continually looks for something to do. When he was younger, he was active in the decision-making groups of the congregation. In recent years, he has not been physically able to participate as much. He misses the ongoing involvement with the business of the church.

He moves slowly and does not now hear very well. His involvement with an adult class studying the Bible used to include leading the group in its study. He is not able to do that any more. Sometimes it is difficult for him to keep track of the discussion but he keeps trying. His attendance in the Bible study group is very regular.

When his wife died of cancer two years ago, he moved in with his daughter. Both his daughter and her husband work away from home. Although George is able to do a few things around the house, he has much empty time on his hands. He sits and watches television much of the time even though he cannot always hear it. Twice a week, he is picked up and taken to be with others in senior citizen programs at the church and in the community. He enjoys being with other people. He has found a friend whose husband died a few years ago. The two of them like being together at the twice-a-week meetings and arrange to be together at other times. Both of them are dependent on others for transportation.

Several of his grandchildren live in the same community. Occasionally they come by to talk with him and ask him to do things with them. They are quite often the ones that give him rides to places he wants to go. One grandson in particular checks with George regularly to see what 'Granddad' wants or needs.

George's eyesight is still good and he is able to continue to read. He shows up at the church for most of the activities and is able to participate. Recently one of the public school teachers who is a member of the congregation remembered George's ability as a carpenter and asked him to work with her class as they made various objects with wood.

During the church service, George occasionally shares out of his experience some wisdom or insight. He is regarded by many of the congregation as one of the 'elders' to whom they listen with appreciation most of the time. Some get impatient with his slow movement and his slow talk. To the children, he is experienced as a gentle old man that some of them find both amusing and interesting.

Grouping People for Learning

The ways in which people are grouped for learning and nurture in the congregation depend on the purpose of the activity, the people involved as both participants and leaders, and the other resources available. A varied program of study and study/action possibilities can be designed to fit the situation of the congregation.

Some possibilities for adults are ongoing church school classes, short-term courses, retreats, book discussion groups, Bible study groups, sermon talk-back sessions, adult forums. Opportunities can be provided for those who work at similar jobs to meet together to consider how they witness to their faith in their daily work or how they deal with the inevitable crises that happen with any job.

Those with children of the same age could meet to work together on the responsibility they share for the education of their children. For instance, groups of those about to have children or with very young children might meet for a period of time as preparation for baptism or infant dedication. They could share how their daily living provides a context within which faith is caught by the very young. A similar set of meetings for those with children ready to begin kindergarten could provide mutual support for sharing the educational task with those in the school system. Another appropriate time for such a group might be at the time when church membership classes are being held for those in early adolescence.

The needs of adults change during the years of their lives. Young adults who are beginning to have practical experience in the working world may be testing various job possibilities, continuing education, developing relationships. For people in middle age, primary meaning in life may flow out of their involvement with their occupations. During middle age, people also must learn to live with their limitations as they come to terms with their inability to fulfill all the dreams of their youth. Older people may have to adjust to failing physical and mental powers, adapting their interests and abilities to the vitality and energy available. Some older people are able to continue active, vigorous lives. For people of any age, it is necessary to consider the unique situation of the people rather than assuming that they fit any stereotype.

Those who marry have different needs and interests than those who do not. In many of our congregations, we assume that only those singles who are young adults need special consideration in our planning. Singles of all ages need affection, personal security and acceptance, companionship on a continuing basis, a sense of meaning and purpose in life. Congregational programming can be done so those who live alone are included.

Those families with children—whether with one parent or two, whether married or not—have needs that shift with the ages and activities of the children. A time of crisis in many marriages happens when all of the children have left home, leaving the couple again alone to work out their patterns and styles of living.

Groupings for youth need to include those of their own age for times of study, action and fellowship. Within the church, adults play a variety of roles with young people of junior high and senior high age. Youth can come to know adults as friends, teachers, learners, role models, co-workers, parents and other adult guarantors. A variety of educational situations can be provided in which youth can relate naturally to adults in these roles.

Youth are eager and ready for experiences beyond the congregation. Camps, retreats, just having fun together can be planned with those of their own congregation, those of different congregations of their own denomination and those of different denominations.

Both children and youth need to have a balance between groups of those their own age and those of other ages. Much time in community with the total congregation is helpful as a context for learning and living the faith.

Occasions in which people of all ages gather happen very often in our congregations. The regular services of worship, times of celebration, picnics and other social activities are among those times. Times for study and/or action that involve all ages—intergenerational education—must be planned with care to be sure that attention is given to the needs of all ages participating. Many adults need to learn that children and youth can teach them as well as learn from them.

The chart on page 104 shows how the Ridgeway Community Church in Harrisburg, Pa., has organized its church school program. Figures across the top are the dates for the Sundays of the year. The boxes show both length of time and the ages of the people in each group. Some of the features of their program are:

(1) Introduction to worship for second and third graders. Since second graders are expected to begin attending services of worship, the fall quarter for the second and third grade is designed to introduce them to different elements of the worship service.

(2) Use of the Bible for fourth and fifth graders. Bibles are presented to fourth grade children on Promotion Sunday each fall. During the fall quarter, the fourth and fifth grade class works on Bible study skills.

(3) Brethren Heritage Series. Brethren heritage materials are used

Proposed 1980 Church School Calendar

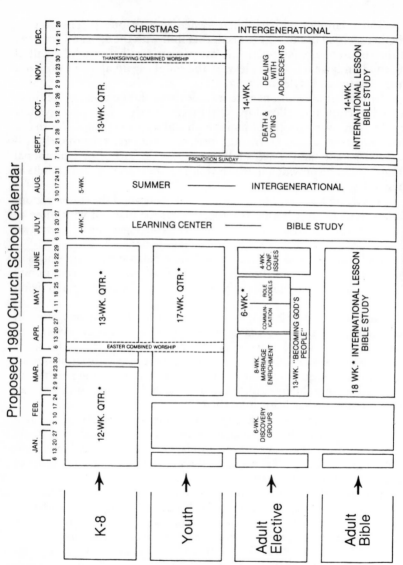

by kindergarten and first grade class through adults for an eight-week series in odd-numbered years.

(4) Intergenerational program. During the summer and again at Christmas, learning experiences involve children, youth and adults in study and worship together.

(5) Combined worship for children and youth. Children and youth have worship together during church school time at Easter and Thanksgiving.

(6) Special summer program. During July and August, special learning experiences adapted to the decreased attendance are planned.

(7) Curriculum for children. Over a two-year period, five of the eight quarters of the *Living the Word* series (a part of *Christian Education: Shared Approaches*) are used for pre-school through grade eight.

(8) Choice for adults. Adults may choose to attend the ongoing Bible study class which uses the International Lessons study guide or the current adult elective classes.

(9) *Becoming God's People* is an adult elective offered each year by the pastor. It is especially for people new to the congregation.

(10) Other education-related activities.

(a) Children's sermons. School children are asked to come forward during worship on the third Sunday of each month from September through June to hear and participate in the children's sermon.

(b) Vacation church school. A weekday church school program is offered for pre-school through sixth grade children with five to ten sessions each August. The program includes worship, study, activities, crafts, games and music.

(c) Youth Club. The weekly after-school program for sixth, seventh and eight graders includes recreation, supper, Bible study and choir practice. Parents of Youth Club members assist with the program.

(d) Pastor's class. A six-session class for sixth, seventh and eighth graders has been offered each spring by the pastor. The class is on the meaning of Christian discipleship. In the future it may be included in the Youth Club program.

(e) Youth groups. The group for sixth, seventh and eighth graders has social events approximately six times a year. The senior high group has two or three meetings a month which include a business meeting, recreation and socializing. Retreats are also part of the program.

(f) Libraries. Each class of kindergarten through eighth grade has a library time during church school time once a month. Books for youth and adults are also available.

(g) Adult study group. About once a year, the pastor leads an evening Bible study class for adults.

All of this information about the education program at Ridgeway Community Church is shared in a booklet which is distributed to the households of the congregation.

CHAPTER SEVEN

Helping Children
Grow in Faith

An Overview

Children in worship, children and death, and children and evangelism are the concerns in this chapter. Other issues related to the nurture of children might have been considered but these are most important to the understandings in this book about the faith, about people and how they grow, and about the church. The concerns chosen relate directly to the three-part aim for education used in this book: helping people relate to the past, the future, and the present.

Children need to participate with the rest of the congregation in worship. The chapter opens with a story of children being with the congregation at worship, then ideas about ways of doing that without disrupting the worship for others are discussed.

Learning about death within a context that is Christian is a crucial dimension of a child's life. The words of 16-year-old Betsy shared a few days before her death explain how the meaning of Easter changed for her through the years of her illness.

The question of the baptism of children is an issue in the section about evangelism and children. A young adult shares how the meaning of baptism was different for her as an older youth than it had been when she was a child. The discussion then develops what it means to people in the congregation that children are not in need of salvation.

Children in Worship

Michelle was five years old. Her brother, Kenny, was eight. About every other weekend they stayed with their father, John, and their step-mother, Faith. On those weekends all of them went to the church for church school and worship.

John and Faith sang in the choir. In order that the choir not lose needed singers to sit with their children in worship, other adults in the congregation volunteered to have Michelle and Kenny sit with them.

One October Sunday, their grandmother, Shirley, was in town. During the fellowship hour between church school and worship, the children came looking for her. Before the three of them left the fellowship hall, Shirley squatted down and asked the children if they knew her rules for being with her in worship.

They said that they did not know. Then they listened politely while Shirley began her list with: "No talking out loud unless it is part of the service."

"But what if I need to go to the bathroom, Grandma Shirley?" asked Michelle.

"Can you open the door by yourself?"

"Of course. I am big enough for that."

"Okay, then, you would not need to ask me anything, would you?"

"You mean, I can go all by myself?"

"Yes."

Then Shirley continued, "Another rule is that you can do whatever you want to do as long as you do not make any noise, do not move out of the space on the seat or under it, and do not stand up in the pew so people behind you cannot see."

The three of them went into the sanctuary and staked out their claim to about six feet of space in one pew.

Kenny stood up with the congregation and followed along with the words of the hymns being sung. He was proud of being able to read them. Michelle stood on the pew, snuggled up next to her grandmother.

When the congregation was sitting, Michelle was content to sit for a while close to Shirley. During the sermon, she collected the four hymnals that were in the racks close by. Then she made a seat on the pew with them. It was just the right height for her to sit comfortably with her feet on the pew. She checked carefully to see that she was not sitting up too high to block the view of those behind her.

The special music in the service was Mr. Martin singing a solo, "This Is My Task," to celebrate his ninetieth birthday that day. As soon as he started to sing Kenny looked up from what he had been working on in his lap. Then he moved to the edge of the pew and listened with complete attention. Michelle had been sitting on the floor. As soon as Mr. Martin started with his cracked elderly voice, she stood up. She leaned over next to Shirley and listened with obvious delight. After he finished his song, Mr. Martin walked slowly back to his seat. Michelle looked up at Shirley and started to say something to her. Then she remembered the rule about not talking. So she just grinned and put her fingers to her lips.

When the service was over, Michelle was almost jumping with excitement. "Oh, Grandma, wasn't Mr. Martin great?" she asked. With her grandmother's agreement that Mr. Martin was indeed great, she told Shirley that she and Kenny would go over to their father's house to play. They said they would play carefully so they would not mess up their Sunday clothes before someone came to open the door of the house so they could change. And please, would Shirley get John and Faith to hurry home with her so the family could eat soon because they were starved?

Children, even very young children, should be with the rest of the congregation in worship. How else can they come to know themselves as part of a community that worships? Even when they are very small, children can sense the closeness of the community whose worship reflects the rest of its life. Many people who study the behavior and learning of children are convinced that participation comes before understanding. So, even if babies and young children are not consciously aware of what is happening in the experience, the youth and adults need to have them present as a symbol of the wholeness of the family of God which includes people of all ages.

Some have talked of the need to train children to be in worship. It may be that instead adults need to be trained to have children in worship with them. Certainly, adults must take the responsibility for having children present in ways that are not destructive of the atmosphere of worship.

Small babies who cry can be taken from the sanctuary. They can then come back when they are quiet again. One of my husband's early memories of church is being taken from worship by his father when he had made noise and being told that he was not to behave in that way in the future. In the congregation into which he had been born, it was assumed that even very small children would be with their parents during worship. Only recently has the move been made to provide alternative activities for children during the worship services of the congregation. The rationale of removing children from worship was that they did not understand what was happening. But who of us really understands what happens to us individually and corporately during a service of worship? Children when they are very young can pick up signals about what is important from those older than they. They can be with older children, youth and adults and experience with them the wonder and mystery that is worship at its best.

In one congregation, adults other than the parents of babies volunteer to take them to worship at least once a month in order that the parents have an occasional chance to have an uninterrupted worship experience. Perhaps the adult caretakers of the babies—fathers, mothers, others—could sit near the back of the sanctuary on the aisles in order that they might come and go with ease, as the needs of the babies dictate. It might even be possible to mark those seats on the aisles as reserved for baby caretakers.

As they get old enough to be off a lap and moving around, more attention needs to be given to the children and their need to be active. Give them space in which to move and limits beyond which they may not go and enforce the limits consistently. Let them have books with pictures, toys and other favorite things that make no noise with which to play.

One man who was elected head of his denomination for a year recalled in a meeting his experience in worship as a child. He had grown up in an Old Order Brethren congregation in which the services were sometimes three hours long. He remembered being taken to worship by his grandmother. She kept a supply of soft mints available. Just before he would get restless, she would give him a mint. She rewarded his good behavior.

Some of us have seen the reverse happening. A child will begin to be noisy or to cry. Then the parent gives the child some candy to stop the noise. That is rewarding disruptive behavior which is not a helpful way of training children to behave in expected ways.

In one family, the parent responsible for their two preschool children each week takes them into the church library to pick up two books each for their browsing during the service. Necessary for that to be possible, of course, is a group of people in the congregation willing and able to create such a library and maintain it. It was also understood in that family that the children were to look at the books, the parents would not read aloud to them. One reason why that was effective was that the parents did read to the children quite often so they had the memory of that experience on which to draw as they looked at the books alone.

Children can participate in parts of the service of worship as they are able to do so. They will be able to hold a hymnal long before they are able to read the words printed in it. As they learn to read they can follow along with the words and eventually be able to sing along with the congregation.

One of the advantages of having a usual order of service in which some elements are repeated each week is that children may be able to participate more. For the Sundays of Lent in one congregation, the same short benediction was sung by the congregation. Many of the children learned to sing it.

Children's choirs are another way in which children can participate with meaning in the service of worship. One children's choir does such a good job and with such joy that it has become a reason why some people have begun to attend the church's service of worship. In that same congregation, the choir has provided one more place in which the Vietnamese refugee children have been able to participate easily.

Some children can read well enough to be readers of the Scripture in congregations where other than those ordained are allowed to be leaders of the congregation at worship. Families, including the children, can be greeters as people arrive for worship. Families have also been asked in some congregations to do the ushering. In one congregation, families are assigned by the month to be ushers and to be greeters, with as many families assigned as necessary to provide the needed number of people.

The pastor of the church was convinced that children needed to be involved in worship. He decided that older children might be able to participate in leadership by reading the Scripture. So he asked fifth and sixth graders to do that.

Each week he would meet with the one who was to read the next Sunday. These sessions were held on Wednesdays after school. The Scripture text was given to the boy or girl on the Sunday one week before they were to be the reader. That way they had a chance to rehearse on their own, if they wanted to do so. The pastor chose the version of the Bible to be used.

He had available a video tape recorder and camera. He used this equipment as a check on his own counseling. He would tape a counseling session with the permission of the people involved and use it to improve his working style.

The video tape was also used in the day care center the church operated during the week. What was recorded from the day care center was used with parents to evaluate the behavior and learning experiences of their children.

On the Wednesday session after school, the pastor would have the video tape camera set up with the lectern in the viewfinder. On the first time with any of the children, he would show them how it worked. Then he would invite the boy or girl to pretend it was Sunday morning in the service. He provided the necessary cue to the child. The person would read. Then together they would look at the video tape of the reading. The young person was able to see what else needed to be done—like holding the head straighter, looking out into the congregation, speaking more clearly. Having the video equipment available provided a self-evaluation tool that helped the children to learn quickly.

Sharing time in the congregation happened at different times during the service. People talked about special joys and concerns, asked the congregation for prayer, introduced guests and family visitors, called attention to happenings in the congregation, the community and the world. Sometimes people walked up to the front and used the microphone, but usually they stood where they were in the sanctuary.

Children sometimes had contributions to make during the sharing time. Marshall, a small six-year-old during whose heart operations the congregation had been in prayer, marched up to the front one Sunday and asked for the microphone on which he announced the arrival of his baby sister.

Ruth, a smiling ten-year-old, was the family member who introduced her visiting grandmother to the congregation. On another Sunday, she introduced two friends from school who were her guests that day. The two friends had been born in India and had recently moved into town.

Children and Death

For the Easter service with the theme "Morning Has Broken," the pastor asked 16-year-old Betsy to tape-record what Easter meant to her. She had been fighting a losing struggle with leukemia for years. She died about ten days after Easter. The tape recording was played at her memorial service. Some of what Betsy said follows:

"Easter for me the past couple of years has meant much pain and sorrow, happiness and change.

"During the summer four years ago I had become sick again and with treatment lost all my hair. So I went through the winter with much fear and unhappiness, wearing a wig and trying to fit back into society.

"So when Easter came I spent all the day before making a special new dress to wear with my special new hair. The day was beautiful and sunny with a little breeze blowing. After the service a friend and I went outside. The feeling was something I will never be able to describe. I felt alive again in the beautiful sunshine with the breeze blowing through my hair.

A feeling of new life and real joy filled me and I felt I knew part of the real meaning of Easter.

"Easter the next year brought sickness again with my first treatment of radiation on Good Friday. On Easter Day I felt miserable, with my eye swollen so badly I was ashamed to be seen. The next day I was again in the University of Chicago hospital to remain for over a month.

"This Easter again finds me sick, but the love of many wonderful friends and family has kept me going. I think I finally proved to myself that God IS love — the beautiful supportive love that is in all these people, each very unique and very special in a different way.

"I do not have the strength to be at church or even in the bright sunshine. But I was given another very special gift this Easter — the gift of life presented to me by a very special cat. My old black cat and I have been through much together the past eight years — my downs when I felt she was my only friend in the world and her kittens that seemed to make her the proudest, happiest cat in the world. This year she again brought me her special gift — four tiny new babies, each so tiny but so perfect. Two tiny little ears and stubby little tails perfectly placed on each one, and even five tiny claws on each tiny foot.

"I have learned much of the meaning of Easter. I know, for instance, why as a little girl I always wanted a new dress for Easter. It symbolized new life after the dark winter and the pain of Good Friday. Easter is a time of change and new life, a time which often brings some sorrow and pain. But the fulfillment, the happiness that it brings also is so much more wonderful. I send my special greetings to each of you. May you also find some special Easter message, whether it be a tiny crocus pushing through the hard ground or a special sparkle in the eyes of a sick loved one."

The flowering of springtime is a very natural reminder of the life/death/life cycle which Easter celebrates in the story of the crucifixion and resurrection. Actually the Easter story must be told in conjunction with the Christmas account in order to be complete. The natural cycle of seed/flowers/fruit/death/seed is a reminder of that reality. It is said that for the Japanese of Nagasaki and Hiroshima, real healing began for them with the blooming again finally of the cherry blossoms. Colored Easter eggs and new clothes are appropriate symbols of this reality in our lives.

Other natural ways of expressing immortality are seen in the life/death/life experience which is shared by humans as well as other living things. This happens biologically in the birth of those of another generation — whether they are born into our own families or not. The recent flurry of interest in determining one's roots is a manifestation of the searching for a sense of continuity with the past and perhaps therefore with the future.

The creativity in the work which we do is another way of experiencing continuity with the past. Such a sense is part of what motivates us to continue to expend our energy in what life demands from us.

All of these ways of talking about and considering death as a normal part of life are helpful for ourselves and for our children. Those of us who call ourselves Christians have a special understanding of the Easter message. We will come back to consideration of that specialness shortly. But first, let us share about another reality we have in common with all other human beings and one which we must share with our children.

Most of us fear death, our own physical death and that of those near us. This fear is evident in our culture. It is seen in our emphasis on youth, on not wanting to appear to get old. Our funeral practices camouflage the reality of death.

Along with the fear of death, we have a fascination with it. Our interest in the violence on television and that which is reported by newspapers, magazines, radio and television is evidence of our fascination. Those reporting on highway conditions speak of 'gaper's blocks' at the location of accidents. We advocate rough sports — boxing, football — as spectators, if not as participants. Who among us has not watched breathlessly the people on the circus high wire? Automobile racing and bullfighting are other manifestations of our fascination with possible death.

Both the fear and fascination with death are evident in the ways in which we talk about death with each other and with children.

Young children do not experience death personally. Their natural self-centeredness prevents this. A child may suffer loss, may feel abandoned, may feel both fear and resentment that someone who has been in their life is no longer there.

We must be careful what we say about death. First, we have to be clear about our own understandings about death. To say to a child that God has taken the dead person away or needs the person more than the child does may only add to the resentment already felt about being left.

To call death "sleep" is also not helpful. We wake up again when we go to sleep. Those who die do not wake up again in this world. Telling a young child that the dead person is asleep may foster fear of falling asleep.

To say that the person has not died but has entered eternal life is beyond the understanding of children. My own belief is that our experiencing of eternal life does not begin with our physical deaths but is part of our present reality. God's realm and our participation in it are part of the reality of our physical lifetimes. Even as I mention eternal life as part of this temporal world, I am not completely clear about what that means.

If all that is what ought *not* to be said to children about death, what is there that can be shared? The basic idea comes from the passage in Romans 14: "If we live, we live to the Lord; and if we die, we die to the Lord. Whether therefore we live or die, we are the Lord's." Or that same idea can be said in other words—God loves people. We are always in God's care. Our love of God and God's love for us strengthens, supports and heals our wounds and our grief. That can be shared with our children, if it is believed by the adults in their lives.

A special dimension is present in immortality for Christians. Through faith, we know that the life/death/life cycle of our human existence is not a burden but a gift from God. The present moments of our lives are more precious to us because we know they will not go on forever. Part of our stance of faith is to be able to live in the present, rejoicing in whatever is given to us by God at that moment.

Another portion of scripture which is mysteriously helpful to me is that in First Corinthians 15:51-55:

> Lo, I tell you a mystery. We shall not all sleep, but we shall all be changed, in a moment, in the twinkling of an eye, at the last trumpet. For the trumpet will sound, and the dead will be raised imperishable, and we shall all be changed. For this perishable nature must put on the imperishable, and this mortal nature must put on immortality. When the perishable puts on the imperishable, and the mortal puts on immortality, then shall come to pass the saying that is written:
> "Death is swallowed up in victory.
> O death, where is thy victory?
> O death, where is thy sting?"

Who among us can say that we really understand in a complete way what that passage means? We receive it with faith in our hearts and our beings more than we do with our head and our brains.

That is not unlike my experience with airplanes. I know that airplanes are too heavy to fly. Just look at how big they are. Anything that big can never get off the ground. That they do fly is against all my experience with things, their weight and their movement. People have explained to me—several times, in fact—about how the air lifts the plane up. Now, really, who can believe that? But it is true. Airplanes can fly. I stake my life on that being true on the average of once a week. I have faith in the flight of airplanes and I act on the basis of that faith.

We need to have experiences within the faith community, within our families and our daily lives that allow us to learn to act in faith. That does not mean that just anything can be told to children as though it were true when it is not. No, we must share with the children and with each other that in which we have faith, that on which we are willing to stake our lives.

How can we do that? We can do it only because we are people of faith. Now, that is really a circular statement — we can act in faith because we are people of faith. Though that may sound incredible, it has been proven through centuries of faith-sustained generations.

As people of faith, we experience God's care and love. The God who created and creates us continues to redeem us from our inadequacies, loves us just as we are, entices us from our human sin, and sustains us in the midst of the deserts of our lives. This happens to us in spite of our turning away from God at times, in spite of our not being faithful to that to which we are called.

Those of us who live out of a faith-story as Christians find assurance in the recollection of the resurrection. While we were — are yet — sinners, Christ died for us. We too have the possibility of lives full of God's grace. We can receive our lives as gifts, not as problems, because Jesus taught us to do that. And what was it that Jesus taught us?

The message that Jesus taught is in the Old Testament in two places. In Deuteronomy 6:5 we are told to love God, and in Leviticus 19:18 we are told to love our neighbors as ourselves. In three of the Gospels it is reported that Jesus put these two ideas together as the great commandment out of which we should live.

In the Deuteronomy 6 passage, clues are given to us as to how we can witness to the truth contained in the passage. It says that the words are to be on our hearts, to be that out of which we live in our daily activities and the basis for all of life's action.

These ideas are to be taught diligently to our children — meaning all children, not just those who happen to arrive on earth through our family line. We are to talk of these truths when we sit in our houses, when we walk around, when we lie down, and when we rise up — and that's most of the time.

The passage goes on to say that we are to put them on our hands so we can always see them, put them between our eyes that others can see them, write them on the doorposts of our houses and gates so even strangers who wander by can know that we know and love the Lord and our neighbor. I am not suggesting that we ought to use the Jewish ways of reminding ourselves of our faith. But we need something like that so we can remember that we love God and our neighbor as they confront us in Jesus Christ.

Loving God and our neighbor are what the Easter message is about. That is the basis of what we can share with each other and with children. That is what Jesus came to teach us. What needs to die in each of us is our selfishness, our greed, our covetousness, our inability or unwillingness to change our ways of life so others can live.

We know that it means to love our neighbor. Jesus told the story of the one who fell among thieves. As reported in Matthew 25, Jesus stated clearly that to love our neighbor is to see the hungry and the thirsty and respond to their needs.

A constant struggle in my life and perhaps in yours is how that love of God and neighbor can be lived out in our time. What does it mean in relation to food, shelter, human rights, oppression, injustice? How do we respond to the poor, the prisoners, the blind, the broken victims of whom Jesus spoke in the synagogue in Nazareth. These concerns are the basis of all of our ministries in the church. All of what we do, if we are to be faithful to that call from Jesus, will grow out of our response to the demand placed upon us in the death and resurrection of Jesus Christ.

This is the faith that we can live out, that with which we face physical death, that we can share with our children—knowing that God is in charge of the universe; we are not.

Children and Evangelism

When she was a young adult, Marj used these words to talk about her experience related to baptism and the church:

"I was baptized at age 12 when the rest of my Sunday school class was. I think it was mostly because my class and my sister were being baptized that year. My parents tried to talk me out of it but I was too young to know that I was too young.

"At age 12, I was allowed to make very few decisions on my own because of my immaturity. Very few choices affecting the rest of my life were made at this time, and rightfully so.

"Somehow, my congregation and my family allowed me to make this decision—the most important decision of my life—at age 12. I had very little understanding of what was involved in the decision. The baptism held very little meaning for me. The message the adults in that congregation gave to me in allowing me to be baptized at that time was that

baptism was not a very important decision. Had they refused to baptize me, I might have learned that one needs to 'count the cost' before making such an important decision. If my commitment was sincere at age 12, waiting until I was older to be baptized would not have weakened that commitment.

"When I was eighteen years old, I came to have an understanding of what participation in the community of faith might mean. I asked to be baptized into the church because my first 'baptism' had really been for me an infant baptism."

In the discussion of witness as a part of the church described in Chapter One, a basic understanding of the connections between our words and our actions was stated. Because our involvement in the church is significant to us, we want others to have that experience. We yearn to have others share in what is nurturing and sustaining for us.

Evangelism as the effort to convince others of the truth of our faith is one way of witnessing. It is sharing the good news of the gospel of Christ. When we invite others to join with us, we must assume that the one being invited understands the significance of the decision being sought.

Sometimes in their zeal that others may share in what they know as truth, people have attempted to convert children. Or children are expected to evangelize others. Neither of these actions are appropriate or responsible ones. Only people mature enough to be aware of the consequences of their decisions and to be able to make commitments and follow through on them are a field and a force for evangelism. Evangelism is not for children.

Children are able to carry out evangelistic tasks in limited ways. Children can and do experience the presence of God in their lives. Children can and do share their faith in meaningful ways. Children may be and often appear to be channels of God's grace. Children can and do witness to God's love through their actions. Children can be encouraged to share their excitement about and interest in learning about God and Christ with their friends. Children, like Ruth in the story above, can and do invite their friends to participate with them in the activities of the church in which they feel welcomed and wanted.

Children are not in need of conversion. They are already saved. Until they are mature enough to know the consequences of their actions, they are innocent. Their salvation, like ours through our mature decisions, is assured through Christ's loving sacrifice on the cross.

When children were brought to Jesus, he blessed them, saying that they were already residents in God's realm. His instruction was that those who heard him should become like little children – not that they should expect little children to be as they are. (Matthew 18:3-4, Mark 10:15, Luke 18:7).

No mention is made of children being baptized in the report in Acts, though both men and women are identified. (Acts 8:12). At several places in the epistles, reference is made to children as having immature and childish thought needing to be outgrown. With maturity, childish ways are to be given up. (I Cor. 13:11). Our maturity is to be measured by the stature of the fullness of Christ when we are no longer children, tossed to and fro and easily influenced by cunning and craftiness. (Eph. 4:13). Even those who are old enough to be teachers are reminded that they need to be taught again the first principles of God's word which is for the mature, those who have their faculties trained by practice to distinguish good from evil. (Heb. 5:12-14). Those who are mature are urged to press on toward the goal for the prize of the upward call of God in Christ Jesus. (Phil. 3:14-15).

Walter Brueggemann, in his book *Belonging and Growing in the Christian Community*, provides helpful clues to what membership in the body of Christ means. He writes of both child dedication and infant baptism being ways of including children in the community and uses the category 'free gracious inclusion' to hold this understanding. Forms and rituals used by our different denominations are all ways of symbolizing the reality of that free gracious inclusion of children in the family of God.

In a similar way, he identifies both believer's baptism and confirmation of baptismal vows as requiring 'responsible personal decision.' In whatever forms it happens, the free gracious inclusion and the responsible personal decision involve the community of faith. He speaks of child dedication and infant baptism both being celebrations of new life, birth events. Believer's baptism and confirmation as celebrations of faith commitment are adult events.

Believer's baptism and confirmation involve a confession of faith, a declaration of loyalty to Christ, and a uniting with the church through the taking of vows. Membership in the Christian church, in this understanding, requires conversion from our self-centeredness to centeredness in Christ.

Confirmation and believer's baptism are celebrations of a convenant with God and the announcement of a covenantal relationship with those of the church. With our vows of membership, we make a commitment to responsible participation in a congregation which witnesses as a servant to God's salvation of the world.

All of what is involved with believer's baptism and confirmation requires conscious, personal decision. No one can do this for another. No force, either direct or indirect, should be brought upon people to make such decisions. Both our conscious and unconscious actions must in no way diminish the voluntary aspects of such decision-making.

Children are included in the fellowship of the congregation and the wider church. They are to be nurtured, loved and taught in the hope and faith that when they are capable of it, they will make an intelligent and complete commitment to Jesus Christ. Their freedom to make that decision is an important element in the faith to which their allegiance is sought.

In these days in this country, young people are required to go to school until they are 16 to 18 years of age. Is preparation for a life of faith less demanding?

The young are encouraged to wait for maturity before getting married. The chance that marriage will not last is greater if the couple is very young when it happens. Is the decision to follow Christ less significant?

One must be eighteen years old to vote for political candidates. Is the decision-making in the Christian community less demanding?

Although young people may earn money before and during their high school years, most are not expected to decide on a major vocational thrust prior to graduation from high school. Decisions about being economically independent are not usually required of the young. Are decisions related to their lives of faith less important?

Children are not expected to be able to make decisions like these. Commitment to Christ involves all of life, with full consciousness of possible alternatives. Children are unconsciously and naturally part of God's realm. Consciousness of the results of our actions and decisions is one measure of maturity. It just does not happen in the very young.

Let us then put away the practices among us that diminish the significance of decision for faith-commitment. Let us no longer assume that children in the sixth grade church school class should automatically be in the pastor's membership class. Let us not forget that children are anxious to please adults whom they love and respect. Children are likely to respond with words and phrases that have little meaning for them if they think that is what adults want them to say. Let us no longer allow our children to be victims of those who practice and encourage child evangelism out of fear or a distorted understanding of both the Christian faith and of children.

Let our ways of living as individuals, as households, as congregations, as a whole people, be those which manifest our convictions about our faith. May our lives be those which are not fearful that our children and youth will leave the church. Rather let us be, in the words of Bethany Theological Seminary professor, Dale Brown, "a joyous and faithful body living and witnessing in such a way as to attract and invite others in, including our own offspring."

The 1972 Annual Conference of the Church of the Brethren adopted a statement on evangelism one part of which includes the words in capital letters below. The expanded notes are mine.

LET OUR EVANGELISM BE . . .

. . . ACTIVATED BY GOD'S LOVE—so our children may come to know, love and honor God.

. . . AFFIRMATIVE IN SPIRIT—so our working with children may be based in faith rather than fear.

. . . OPEN AND INCLUSIVE—so our children may know that God loves all people, including them.

. . . VARIED IN ITS EXPRESSION—so our children may experience the magnificence of God's world and our various faithful responses.

. . . RESPECT THE INTEGRITY OF INDIVIDUALS—so our children may be nurtured to mature faith decisions based on realistic awareness of possible alternatives and are not forced to premature assent.

. . . FORTHRIGHT IN ITS PROCLAMATION—so our children may hear our words of witness, obviously reflecting our dependence on God, our following of Christ, and our nurture by the Holy Spirit.

. . . INCARNATED IN PERSONS—so our children may know and love many people who know and love them, as God loves us all.

. . . INCORPORATED IN ACTIONS—so our children may participate with us in deeds of loving service.

. . . EXTENDED THROUGH THE HOME—so our children may have a secure base from which to venture forth on their own pilgrimages of faith.

. . . FACILITATED THROUGH THE CHURCH—so our children may experience themselves as a part of a faithful community worshipping God and witnessing to God's love and grace.

III.
Critical Issues in
Education and Nurture

CHAPTER EIGHT

Teaching That Enables

An Overview

In Chapter Four, the fact that all of life educates us was discussed. In this chapter, the focus is on those learning experiences for which we plan.

The first of three stories tells how children in one congregation challenged those older than they to demonstrate that those older did indeed know from memory that which the children were being asked to learn. How a nearly-blind girl is able to participate with the rest of the class is the next story. The third story is of an intergenerational learning experience.

Ingredients or dimensions of learning experiences which must be considered in planning are language, human relationships, images, values and tools. Ideas about each of these is shared in this section.

The descriptions of people in Chapter Six are used to suggest teaching approaches for people of different ages. The emphasis is on those methods which might be helpful in accomplishing the intended aim of education in the church—people linked with the past, anticipating the future and participating responsibly in the present—within a context that is Christian.

Young people and adults were lined up in the hallway outside the classroom where the third and fourth graders met. The people coming out of the room each carried a small sheet of paper.

In the room, the members of the third and fourth grade class were seated at tables. In front of each was a sheet of paper. The youth and adults would come in and sit down across from one of the class members. Then each of these visitors to the class would recite the names of the books of the Bible in order. Next, they would write their names down on the sheet of paper and receive from the third or fourth grade child a note stating what they had done.

This activity went on from 9:15 to 9:30 a.m. for four weeks. During that time, 20 senior high youth and about 150 adults had put their names on the lists in the third and fourth grade classroom. Also on the lists of those who knew the names of the books of the Bible in order were most of the third and fourth graders.

The teaching material for the third and fourth grade class had suggested in the first session of the quarter that the children might learn the books of the Bible in order. When this possibility was considered by the children, they had two questions for their teachers:

"Why do we need to do this?" asked one.

The teacher in charge asked the class to think of reasons why it might be helpful to know the books of the Bible in order. After some consideration, they decided that it would help them to be able to find references easier.

The next question was, "Do the adults in the church know the books of the Bible in order?" The teacher replied that he did not know. Out of their conversation around this point, the decision was made to invite those in senior high and older to demonstrate to the class members if they did have such knowledge.

Such a good feeling developed of everyone learning together that those responsible for planning for education in the congregation decided to ask one class between kindergarten and grades seven and eight to issue a similar invitation each quarter. During the first year, in addition to learning or relearning the names of the books of the Bible, the youth and adults demonstrated their knowledge of the Twenty-third Psalm, the Lord's Prayer and the Ten Commandments. The challenge relative to the Ten Commandments came from the junior high group during the quarter they were studying that set of rules from the Old Testament.

Susan was not quite blind. She could see black outlines on a sheet of paper. The fifth and sixth grade class of which she was a member was making stained-glass designs with the symbols of the church on them. During such projects, she would put out her hand and ask for a black crayon. With that she drew her design with heavy lines. With her left hand, she could feel the crayon marks. Then she would ask for a colored crayon to fill in between the black lines. She asked someone else to do the ironing of her design between two sheets of waxed paper.

The American Bible Society had provided her with the Bible in Braille. One of the teachers of the class would call Susan on Friday or Saturday each week to tell her which piece of the Bible she should bring with her. Then Susan could participate in the unison readings or take her turn in reading.

During one vacation church school, she brought her Brailler and name cards for everyone in the group. Then each put his or her name on the card in what Susan called 'plain writing' so those who could see would also know who they were.

One time the group was beginning to work on a choral reading. Someone asked if they could tape-record it. So the first time through a tape was made. When it was played back, it sounded garbled and difficult to understand. They played the same tape again. This time Susan began to laugh. She said that she had gotten mixed up and was reading in the wrong place and did not come in at the right times. She agreed to memorize her parts of the reading for the next day. The tape they made that day was all right.

Susan had a brother just younger than she who was also going blind. He was angry about his situation, so the efforts to work with him in similar ways did not work. He quit coming to the church school class.

The life-style assessment study/action group included people from nine families. For the meeting just before Easter, they decided to invite others in their families to participate with them in an intergenerational learning experience.

The group who gathered ranged in age from pre-school into the mid-sixties. The participants included:

—a woman who has never married who brought a woman friend as her family.

—a woman born in China married to a man born in India and who was alone because their children are all grown and he was away on a trip.

—another woman alone was formerly married with her family all grown.

—a family of four with one in junior high and the other in senior high.

—a family of five, one in elementary and two in junior high.

—a couple near retirement.

—a couple with neither of their college age youth with them.

—a recently married young couple who are vegetarians.

—a couple with their four college-age young people home for spring *break.*

—a woman with five adopted children of ages four through fifteen, all of mixed racial parentage, without her husband who was at home with another child who was sick.

The salad for the meal was created out of parts brought by each family. The cost of the macaroni and cheese was shared by all.

Families had brought an egg for each family member to decorate. Supplies of all kinds and some elementary instruction in the use of some of them were provided. After the eggs had been decorated, each displayed his or her creation and told a story to the rest about it.

After the meal, the group was divided into five groups of six people each. The assignment was that each group pretended to have $100 to spend for a week's vacation for their created family of six. Each created family could use whatever resources—like cars and bikes—that actually belonged to the people in the group. Members of the multi-racial family of six were in four of the five groups. The family owned a van. So each of those four groups decided that they would use the van to transport them for biking or camping as their activities during the vacation. One of those groups decided they would go fishing and catch fish so they would have more money available for gas and could go farther away. The group without the van did have bicycles, so they decided to stay at home for their vacation and make one-day trips around the area.

After the groups had done their planning, they gathered in a large circle to share their plans. The group laughed at and with the family intending to feed themselves on their fishing. After the sharing, they sang some songs. After sharing in a prayer, they all went home.

Ingredients of Learning

The ingredients or dimensions of teaching experiences are language, human relationships, images, values and tools. When we do not think very deeply about teaching and learning, it might seem that language is used more in formal teaching times while tools are used more in those unplanned times when learning happens. This is not so. All of the dimensions are involved in most learning experiences. That being the case, the teaching and nurturing for which we plan needs to take into account all of these ingredients.

Language

Language includes not only words but also symbols, such as the cross, and signs such as @*#&%($). All of these are abstractions from reality which allow us to deal with life. Language is a product of culture.

When one travels in a place where people speak a language unknown to the traveler, the reality of this cultural base is obvious.

We cannot assume that even those who might be able to speak English as we do will understand or make sense out of the message we are sending. In the introduction to his book, *The Image,* Kenneth Boulding describes the difficulty of communicating, of sending and receiving messages. The message being sent may not be received at all. It may have no meaning to its intended recipient. If it makes sense to the person, then it either adds to what is already known or changes it in some way. We cannot be sure that the words, signs and symbols we use will mean the same to someone else as they do to us.

For instance, I grew up in a family that did not relate much to the church. I began participating regularly in a congregation at the age of twenty. Many of the words, signs and symbols of the Christian faith had little if any real meaning for me. Bread used during communion apparently meant more to other participants than it did to me. Words like sin, salvation and grace had little meaning. It was obvious that others around me were operating out of some understanding that I did not have. My husband and others assumed that I knew much that I did not. We discovered this to be true when I was enrolled in seminary as a middle-aged wife and mother. I would come home all excited about something newly learned about the faith. I would ask my husband if he knew some particular fact, concept or image that I had just learned about our faith as Christians, saying, "What I found out today was . . . " His surprised response was, "Did you not know that already, Shirley?"

The interaction between experience and learning is complex. It seems to be the case that we learn out of experience. Certainly our language is dependent upon experience. Fifteen years of life in a congregation provided the experience out of which the teaching I got at seminary made sense. The reflection in that setting on my experience was that which turned the experiencing into learning for me.

Since learning grows out of our experience, we need to plan our teaching situations so that the words, signs and symbols we use have meaning to those we are trying to teach. Language which comes to have meaning is that which is used. The cross, the Bible, the elements of communion will be seen and experienced as having importance and special significance to adults before their meaning is understood by children.

Relationships

Human relationships are an important ingredient in the learning process. Our teaching has a double strength to it when the content is consistent with the style in which it is done. If we are trying to teach that people are a significant part of God's creation and each is a unique, unrepeatable gift from God to the world, those we teach are not likely to learn that if we are unable to call them by name.

Human interaction is evident in each of the stories. In the memorizing situation, the involvement of the children with those older than they was a significant part of the learning experience. In that same story, the teacher's being willing to say that he did not know something could help the children experience him as a human being not unlike themselves. In the story about Susan, her willingness to risk herself and the group's acceptance of her affirmed her as the partially-sighted person she was. The possibility that people of several decades in age can learn together was basic to the session of the lifestyle group.

Images

Images are an ingredient in learning just as they are in all of life. Boulding identifies some of his own images as being . . .

. . . images of space held with words like global, galaxy and universes that tell him where he is,

. . . images of time that go back to the formation of the earth and into the future so he knows when he is,

. . . images of personal relations that tell him to some extent who he is,

. . . images of nature that provide him with a world of how things operate,

. . . and images that include a world of subtle intimations and emotions.

All of us carry similar pictures in our heads, though the details of those images are multiple and complex. We have pictures of ourselves which are often not very flattering and which sometimes get in the way of our effectiveness. The pictures of our worlds are distorted by our experiences. Often our pictures of other people put them in categories like boxes which get in the way of our relationships. Our pictures of the church may or may not strengthen us.

Our images of time, space, things, people and relationships shift according to our situation. Think a bit about how long a distance is when you are walking as contrasted with the same distance when you drive it in a car. Or consider how an amount of time spent doing some monotonous work seems longer than the same time when having a joyous time with a beloved friend.

Values

Values are present in the midst of learning just as they are in all of life. Some people are able to develop multiple, flexible systems of values which can be changed. Some values are more or less inflexible from the viewpoint of Christians—values like justice, mercy, love, care, nurture, responsibility, accountability, covenant and peace—though what those words mean and the images that hold them will vary greatly among us.

Our values are constantly under pressure to change. Much of the uneasiness in our lives today has to do with the apparent shifting of some of the basic values of a former time. We are not sure anymore about what being a family is, what loving another means, what equality requires, what justice for all implies, and so on. We are often not even aware of the values which we hold strongly. Our nurturing structures at home and in the congregation can help us to become conscious of our values in order that we can affirm them as real and true for us, or change those which we discover in ourselves that are not what we want for ourselves and others.

The stories provide illustrations of many values. The children felt that if those older than they were able to demonstrate their knowledge, then it must be important for them to acquire that same information. Susan's teachers held the value of providing the possibility for everyone in the group to participate. A value evident in the lifestyle group was that each, regardless of age, was able to contribute to their learning experience.

Tools

The tools for teaching and learning can be as complex as a computer or as simple as a piece of chalk. Materials for working with ideas and concepts are a necessary part of the learning process. The stick which Jesus used to write in the dust was a learning device to those about to stone the woman. Complex tools like typewriters, adding machines, mini-computers, video-cassette equipment, films and so on are among the tools that are available in general education situations.

Some of the tools identified or implied in the stories include paper, pencils, newsprint charts, Bibles, newssheets or other ways of issuing the invitation to demonstrate their memories, curriculum materials, tables, chairs, magic markers, crayons, waxed paper, boiled eggs, shared food, the Bible in Braille, the Brailler, name cards, tape recorder, tape, telephone and so on.

Teaching Approaches for People of Different Ages

Many resources are available to help those working in congregations do learning activities of various kinds. The particular focus of this section is related to the stated aim for education: to help people of all ages develop and maintain linkage with the past, to anticipate the future and to participate responsibly in the present. The discussion here then will center on such questions as:

How can people learn who they are?

How can they remember who they are?

What enables people to move into the future realistically?

In what ways can people learn to participate in the decision-making about their own lives?

In order to answer such questions, we need to consider what values, skills, attitudes and concepts are needed from the accumulated wisdom of the church, from the Bible, from the world around us and from our own ongoing personal situations? Much of the content of this book has been speaking to this issue. All of section I dealt with the context in which people are living. In section II, descriptions of people of various ages has been provided. Now in this first chapter of section III, our attention can be turned to the methods of teaching which will produce the desired results—people linked into the past, anticipating the future and participating responsibly in the present.

In each of the age group sections following, names are given. These refer back to the descriptions in Chapter Six.

Young Children—Todd, age 2; Sarah, age 5

Young children like Sarah and Todd live in the here and now. We do not deal directly about the future with them. They can be nurtured in ways that do not destroy their imaginations or their sense of the fantastic. Let them indulge their imaginations without having to operate out of an adult's sense of what is right or wrong. Who is to say that trees must be green or the sky must be blue? In the story in Chapter Seven, Michelle's use of the hymn books to make herself a seat during worship was evidence of her creative imagination.

Encouraging children to live fully the moment at hand can provide a secure base for projecting both into the past and into the future when their sense of time has developed. It is also an appropriate way for people of all ages to respond. So often we miss the joy of the present in our guilt about the past or our anxiety about the future. The present is the gift God gives us over and over again. Maybe the ability to play, to be lost in the delight of the moment is what Jesus meant when he said that we should become like little children. (Matthew 18:3-4, Mark 10:15, Luke 18:17).

Being called by name, being identified as part of a family, being welcomed by people as a valuable human being are all ways of providing security and a healthy self-image to children. Out of such security can come the self-assurance from which we can move into love of neighbor and of God.

Participation in worship provides young children the opportunity to experience the sights, sounds and rhythms of worship. Being in the warm embrace or sitting close to another person reinforces the child's sense of belonging, of being wanted. It is more important for children to see their parents and others at prayer and at worship and using the Bible often than it is for them to be told about prayer or expected to learn the content of the Bible.

Probably the most valuable contribution to learning for young children is that they have the opportunity to play, to be with others in warm and loving situations. It has been said that play is the work of children. It is certainly a means by which they experiment with various ways of responding to life.

At the same time, children at a very young age can learn what is appropriate behavior for differing situations and to honor the rights and dignity of other human beings. Our experiences with children can provide occasions in which they learn in these ways.

Older Children—Mike, age 9

Children are able quite young to understand rules and standards of behavior. They learn early to take turns in their play. They soon learn that they can create rules, handle conflict and make plans for their own learning. They do all of these, even outside of formal class situations.

As children see parents and other adults working in the church, they come to know what is involved in being part of community and family. Care needs to be taken, therefore, that some jobs in the church and in the family are not seen as less worthy than others. Leadership and decision-making obviously need to be carried by many people rather than just a few. In both the congregation and the household, children need to experience ways in which everyone contributes to the care of others.

Helping children to work through their own conflicts as much as possible is good learning. It is so easy for adults to intrude into situations and be either too permissive or too authoritarian. Procedures can be used that have limits as well as possible choices in them as a way of developing the ability to make appropriate decisions.

Use ways of teaching that insist that children be active learners rather than passive receivers of information. We become thinkers, planners and actors by thinking, planning and acting. Encourage the children to talk about what they do in their daily lives. Help them to see that the stories about what they do also tell who they are and who they are becoming.

Youth—Becky, age 13, Joe, age 17

Through their idealism, many young people project into the future with more ease than those of other ages. They have not yet had experience in the work world which limits their dreaming. Peter's Pentecost speech about the young seeing visions and the old dreaming dreams speaks to the issue of maintaining linkage with the past and anticipating the future.

Relating to the old who are dreaming dreams is appealing to some of the young. Apparently, some youth are willing to listen to people the age of their grandparents more than to those the age of their parents. This may be a natural way of maintaining continuity with the past. Perhaps the youth can listen to the elders with more sensitivity because no authority or power issue is involved as there is with those the age of their parents.

Young people enjoy and learn from work projects in which they can demonstrate their competence alongside adults. The sensitivity and idealism of youth can be shared through their participation in worship as worship leaders and in individual and small group sharing. Youth are ready to serve in most of the ways adults do in the congregation, but they need to have escape hatches when adult responsibility becomes too heavy for their maturity.

Young people can be led to consider alternative ways of group decision-making besides voting. Sometimes a consensus style can be used in which the viewpoints of all present are represented in the final decision. In voting, quite often a minority of the people must submit to the will of the majority.

At a national youth conference, the senior highs did simulations of the denomination in its annual decision-making meeting. The youth conference was held just before and near the site for the denominational annual meeting. Out of the simulation came the decision to send representatives from their youth meeting to the group which reviews the business of the conference for the delegates from congregations.

The question sent with the youth delegation to the business reviewing group was, "How could a person under twenty years of age be elected to the decision-making board of the church?" They were told that such a person would need to be nominated either by being on the ballot presented ahead of time or by nomination from the floor when the ballot was presented. Advance permission of the nominee was necessary.

When the delegation reported back to the youth meeting, it was decided that they should nominate one of their body from the floor. As a result of their work, a young person was elected for a three-year term. Only when the youth knew what was possible were they able to participate responsibly.

Adults—Bob/Mary, age 24; Cathy, age 53; George, age 75

Although the portraits of adults of different ages in Chapter Six intend to show some of the differing needs that ebb and flow during adulthood, the methods with which we are concerned here may be appropriate for all adult groups. For example, adults of all ages probably need help in receiving the present with joy as well as maintaining hope for the future.

A natural shift with increasing age appears to happen between young adulthood that is oriented toward the future and later adulthood that focuses on the past. One of the crises that can develop in middle age is the realization that the dreams of youth and young adulthood are not likely to be fulfilled. All of us need help in maintaining our connections with the past, in anticipating the future and in participating in the present. Skills, attitudes and concepts in these areas can be learned. The style of life in the household and in the congregation are powerful factors in that learning.

One attitude that can be learned is that of cooperation, dialogue and empathy. People can learn to keep lines of communication open. They can practice the testing of their operating rules and values, retaining those that continue to have relevance but changing others. Through their involvement in groups in the church, people can become acquainted with new ways of responding to their lives and can practice those responses until they become natural and easy to do.

Learning to participate responsibly is more likely to happen when the groups in which people find themselves operate in an open and inquiring style rather than a closed and dogmatic one. Having more rather than a few people involved in leadership roles of all kinds engenders such a sense of openness. More is said on this in the chapter about recruiting, training and supporting leaders.

Intergenerational education

Occasions in which people of all ages gather happen very often in the congregation. The regular services of worship, times of celebration, picnics and other social activities are among those times. Occasions for study and/or action that involves all ages—intergenerational education—must be planned with care to be sure that attention is given to the needs of all ages participating. Adults need to learn that children and youth can teach them as well as learn from them. Children and youth need to know themselves as teachers as well as learners.

Many of our children grow up in the congregation with their parents assuming that they know the names of the adults of the congregation. The children of the congregation may hear the adults talk to and about others but not know the people to whom the names refer. That is more likely to happen in congregations in which most activity is done only with one's own age group or where activity is largely adult-centered.

To be able to call one another by name is only one of the reasons for planning for intergenerational education. In such educational experiences the young can observe and know those who are struggling with the issues of faith. From those older than they, the young can learn the history of God's continuing encounter with human beings. This can happen through the sharing of personal experiences and of understandings about the Bible, the church and the world. In turn, the young can remind those older of the fresh approach experienced in the questions which young people bring to their involvement with life.

Because people respond to life in so many various ways, intergenerational educational experiences provide a rich source for models of discipleship. One of the ways in which we learn that we do not hold all of the same principles central in our lives is to know people of conviction who do not share the same views of the world and the demands of the gospel. Intergenerational education can focus on some dimension of the church's life and work, the world in which we live, the heritage of the Bible and the church or personal needs and interests, in a setting that allows those kinds of understandings to be expressed.

One way of learning that life is open and full of possibilities is to participate in learning experiences with people of all ages who represent various styles of response to life—all of which can be seen as faithful responses. The congregation is literally a repository of gifts and fruits of the Spirit. Intergenerational education provides one means of discovering, celebrating and sharing those gifts and fruits.

CHAPTER NINE

A Model for
Effective Organization

An Overview

A critical issue in both households and congregations is organizing to get the work done that is necessary to maintain those institutions. The story at the beginning of the chapter tells how one family organized itself to accomplish the necessary tasks, enabled everyone to participate in decision-making and celebrated events in the lives of the members of the household. Questions are raised about who does what in the households of the congregations. These stories and ideas are shared because it is assumed that the process of getting work done is similar in households and congregations.

Two stories are told about recruiting, training and supporting teachers in the congregation followed by some ideas about these same issues. In the family stories and ideas, people were involved in doing various tasks and performing certain functions. The stories from congregations are similarly about people learning to be more productive or more effective in their tasks.

Some ideas are shared about what needs to be done in most congregations in relation to worship and in relation to education programs. The need for and ideas about how to support teachers are included in this section.

Earl and Shirley went to a weekend learning experience designed to help individuals and families organize their lives around the concept of covenant in a missional context. In the first session, they considered meanings of the word 'covenant' and each family unit began to work on a family constitution. In the second and third sessions, they worked on organizing their households to get the necessary work done and on developing a budget which would reflect their desired priorities. In the final session, plans were made for family celebrations and educational experiences. Each family unit created a family symbol which was shared with the whole group.

As a result of that experience, Earl and Shirley met with members of their family for a day-long work session the next weekend. Several changes were made in their family life. It was agreed that household tasks would be shared by all. A family meeting would be held each week, usually on Sunday afternoon following the noon meal.

One of the patterns for the family meeting included the following elements:

Announcement that the Heckman family meeting was in session.

1. To deal with the past

a. Conversation on what had happened during the previous week—individually, in the community, the country, the world.

b. Accountability and absolution. Two kinds of questions were possible to ask during accountability depending on the preference of the one leading the meeting that day: Questions of specific accountability like 'Have you done your job this week?' or 'Did you attend worship this morning?' are relatively easy to answer with a simple yes or no. Questions of general accountability that are never completely done or not done must necessarily be answered either 'yes and no' or 'no and yes' because such mixed answers are the only possible response to a question like: 'Have you been faithful to the mission of this family this week?'

Then, because it is the way God treats us, Christians know that a word of absolution is always said on the other side of accountability. God's judgment is always in the context of God's mercy. Through spoken words of absolution, we are reminded that nothing we do can either gain or lose us the love of God.

2. To respond to the present

a. Complaints and compliments. For a period of time, Anita regularly complained that Alan was her brother. That public announcement apparently released her to get along with him very well. If complaints that could be remedied persisted over a period of time, some action was suggested to change the situation.

b. Celebrations of birthdays, getting a driver's license, receiving report cards, getting a traffic ticket, and so on. It was in a family meeting that John announced his engagement to Kathy. On one occasion, Earl's no longer having a job was a moment for family celebration during this part of the meeting. The work that Earl had found when the family moved from Denver was dependent on there being special assignments and sufficient jobs in the office to keep him busy. After being in that office for nearly a year, the work ran out. The next Sunday, Anita who was almost thirteen years old was chairing the family meeting. When it came to celebration time, Anita looked over at her mother and asked: "How do we celebrate Dad not having a job anymore, Mom?"

Before her mother could answer, Anita decided that the family could do it just like birthdays. So she asked Earl questions like: 'What was significant about this past year of work for you, Dad?' Among the things he shared was that it had been good to be able to walk home for lunch and it had been a relief not to have all the extra work that went with being your own boss. 'What seems important to you as you look ahead into the future?' He talked then about his concern in looking for a job at 54 years old, his decision to wait for the couple of months to look for a position until he had heard whether he had passed the engineering registration exam in Illinois. He also said that perhaps something new might come into being for him professionally.

    3. To deal with the future

      a. Schedule for the next week. A chart was filled out with space for the activities of each family member still at home. At one time in the family history, it looked like this:

WEEK OF:							
✕	M	T	W	T	F	S	S
EARL							
SHIRLEY							
ALAN							
ANITA							

      b. Jobs for the next week. It had been decided that three sets of tasks needed to be done by each team of two people:

    Team 1 did the laundry and the bookkeeping. Each family member would sort his or her part of the laundry into marked boxes. The team members washed and dried the laundry and returned it to its designated *storage space. Personal items were picked up in the laundry room. Doing the bookkeeping helped all members of the family learn to write checks and know details of the family's financial situation.*

Team 2 cleaned up the kitchen after meals, tidied up the common living areas of the house and did the yard work.

Team 3 planned the meals, purchased the food and cooked the meals.

Each week, the teams shifted to the next job with everyone taking turns doing all the work. Variations in both jobs and ways of assigning people shifted over the years. A time came when John participated only occasionally in the regularly assigned tasks. This was due partly to his outside job schedule, but also perhaps because he was nearing independent adulthood when the shift was made from when Shirley was the household manager to the cooperative approach.

When a French foreign student came to live with the family three years after they had initiated the shared approach, he was told that part of living in that family was taking his turn in doing jobs. He was also expected to keep his own room clean, including changing the sheets and delivering them to the laundry room on the right day. He did not like the idea of doing such work and had never been expected to do so before. He decided to risk staying with the family instead of transferring to another one. He did participate as one of the team members, learning to work as well as the others did. It was very amusing to the whole family when one of the celebrations was Herve's getting a job working in a pizza place run by German folks. He and they could speak both French and German to each other while many of their customers were more fluent in Spanish than in English.

The team structure did not always work. Sometimes the cleaning did not get done. Earl and Cindy were more conscientious about doing their share of the work than the others. It would go along for a while with people not doing their tasks. Then an explosion of tempers would have the operation running again for another short term.

    c. Send-out for the week

Besides the family meeting with the structures within it, there were other results from the first attempts at participatory family life. Longer-range planning was done. More care was taken about what the decor in the house communicated.

Twice a year, the family had a planning session at least an afternoon long. During that time, the expenses for the past six months were reviewed and the budget checked for the next six months. Plans for vacations, other trips and for schooling were discussed in these sessions.

*As the younger generation began to leave, it got increasingly dif-
ficult to maintain the team structure. When the family moved from
Denver with the two younger ones in seventh and ninth grades and the
two older ones gone, they began to do jobs as individuals, with
assignments being related to increasingly complicated employment and
work schedules.*

The story of one family's ways of organizing itself for mission is told
here as a hint of what is possible for households to do, given the right
context and some tools. It is also possible that the elements of that
family's structure provide a model for what needs to happen in congregations to get the work done in a style consistent with the aim of church
education and nurture stated several times already in this book — that
people maintain linkage with the past, anticipate the future and live
responsibly in the future.

In this section, we consider first some questions or activities that
might lead you to think about your own family situation or that might be
designs that could be used in family-education situations in the congregation. Then we will look at a model for congregational life derived from
the family's style as told in the story.

From the list below check the activities that need to be done in your
household. Add others that are unique to your family and not on the list.
By each item checked, put the initials of the one in your household who is
currently doing that job.

_____ earn money
_____ plan for meals
_____ buy food
_____ prepare food
_____ clean up after meals
_____ provide ongoing care for infants or very small children
_____ provide after-school supervision for children
_____ do laundry
_____ clean areas of the house used by all people
_____ clean own living spaces
_____ plan for the future of the family
_____ keep financial records
_____ do income tax
_____ plan for schooling of children
_____ plan for retirement
_____ plan for family vacations
_____ consider future educational plans for any family member

_____ mow yard
_____ tend the garden
_____ deal with the produce from the garden
_____ shovel the snow
_____ walk the dog
_____ plan for family celebrations
_____ entertain friends
_____ maintain the kin network—with letters, visits, etc.
_____ consider involvement of family members in activities in church, community, etc.

_____
_____
_____

_____

Or try a different approach. List the members of your household. With each name, list the jobs and the roles performed. For instance:

Earl - meal cleanup
    - gardening and dealing with the produce
    - yard work
    - making bread and granola
    - serving as the stable center of family life
    - getting own meals when Shirley is away
    - earning two-thirds of the family income

Consider the equity of the job activity in your household which your listing indicates. Are some tasks only the work of women? Are some tasks only done by men? Are the children, if any, given significant assignments.

What changes in assignment of people to do jobs might be considered? What jobs in the household need to be done by everyone so no one feels like a servant of the others? For instance, cleaning the toilets is one job nobody likes to do but it must be done. Maybe taking turns at toilet-cleaning and learning to do that job well would be more equitable. Consider what changes are needed in order that each person in the household has an opportunity to care for the others in the family in such a way that no one experiences himself or herself as less than other household members.

In the household of the story, the situation has shifted over the thirty years of its existence at this writing. Changes have occurred in the almost fifteen years since Earl and Shirley went to that course. More changes are likely to occur in the future. What has happened in your household recently to prepare you for the inevitable changes that come with the changes in age of both the first and second generations of people of the household?

In their helpful book *The Intentional Family*, Jo Carr and Imogene Sorley describe the responsibility of parents for the second generation as being to "accept . . . expect . . . enable . . . discipline . . . launch" the children. They go on to suggest specific helps to guide the family in working through some of the issues that are being raised here.

Who Does What in the Congregation?

The congregation had a single class for grades two through six. Each year they had three adults working with the group of children. From twelve to twenty children were in the group. Two adults might have been enough to handle the situation. However, with three it was possible each year to have a new person who previously had not worked with children to experiment with the possibility of being a teacher. With three, it was also always possible to have two adults present when one needed to be away. Ordinarily, all three were present.

During his first year of working with the class, Frank was a very assistant assistant teacher. He met with the other two teachers to do planning each week. He prepared worksheets and was willing to work with the small groups as they did projects such as creating a mural. He was not willing to do anything that would have him up in front of the whole group doing what he called 'teaching.' When asked what he was doing, if it was not teaching, he replied that he was 'helping the others to teach.'

In his second year, he and one of the other two teachers continued to work with the children. Now another was newer at the task than he was. He began to be willing to read a story, lead the group in prayer and take other assignments, knowing that he was not going to be the only adult present at any time.

By the third year that he worked with the children (which was the longest period of time anyone in the congregation was allowed to do so), Frank had acquired enough self-confidence that he was able to lead discussions and be one who was interactively involved with the young ones.

Frank talked about how his experience with the children's class had helped him understand much about the Christian faith. During the three years that Frank worked with the children, no meetings of all of the congregation's teachers were held nor was there any congregational training available. He with others from the congregation had participated each of the three years in the local interchurch training sessions held for six Sunday evenings in the fall. He said that in those sessions he had learned much about the Bible and theology as well as information and understandings related to the teaching he was doing.

The congregation had about sixty children in kindergarten through grade eight. Enough children of each age group were available to have age-group classes. But instead, they decided to have a learning center style with the children of those ages in order that learning could be individualized and they could provide many avenues of learning for them.

Two kinds of teachers were recruited. One set were the content providers. They told stories, created dramas, arranged for audio-visuals. They worked with all of the children, but for short periods of time. The other kind of teachers were continuity providers and those with special skills who worked with the children in various centers.

Each quarter, one group of teachers was working with the children and having a meeting once a week to work through the detailed planning needed. At the same time, the teachers who had been recruited to work the next quarter were also meeting each week. They were studying the content of the quarter's work, deciding how to work with the children on that content, and preparing for the next quarter. In that congregation, you could be recruited to be a teacher for one quarter, 13 Sundays at a time, knowing that you would be expected to have one evening meeting each week for the 13 weeks prior to beginning to work and one evening meeting for each of the 13 weeks you were teaching.

The expectations were clear. The assignment was for a limited period of time. Testimony from those who worked in the learning center was that it was a good learning experience for them. The congregation had no trouble securing enough adults to help with the learning center. They had a waiting list of people with special skills willing to share them — storytelling, photography, drama, music, and so on.

In the senior high youth group of that congregation, the ninth to twelfth graders had a variety of needs and interests. With the help of their adult leaders, the youth decided that they should also have a variety of possibilities for learning available to them as did the children.

Each quarter, two of the young people were allowed to work in the learning center during church school time. The list of those who wanted to do this was long, even though they were expected to participate in the same way as the others who worked as learning center enablers. This meant a commitment of one night a week for six months as well as the involvement on Sunday mornings for three months.

Another choice available to the youth was to participate in the ongoing Bible study led by the pastor on Sunday mornings. Only those who had studied the assigned material were allowed to participate in the *discussions. The room was set up with crepe paper streamers dividing the alcove where the Bible study took place from the rest of the room. In the other part of the room were bookshelves containing mostly second-hand books as well as some specially-chosen volumes, pillows on the floor, table games, and a very relaxed atmosphere.*

A third choice available to the young people was that they could be in that part of the room, doing anything they wanted to do except make noise which would be distracting to those in Bible study. Some of the group were regularly in the Bible study group. Some were never in the Bible study group. Others moved back and forth through the crepe paper curtain, being sometimes in the study group and sometimes not.

Getting the work done at church is similar to the same task in a household. The process is the same. An analysis needs to be done of what is needed. An estimate is made of who is available to do what is needed. The two — needs and abilities — are then matched together. Often in the congregation and sometimes in the household, it is assumed that only certain people are able to do certain jobs. That may be the case in a few instances. Being able to read directions in order to operate equipment or do some kinds of cooking may be examples from the home situation. But even then, the person not able to read can be put on a team with one who can.

In the congregation, other kinds of examples come to mind. Being able to sing on key and follow the direction of the choir leader are necessary to be in the adult choir in many churches. Probably all children and youth who want to be should be permitted to be in choirs for the people of their ages.

Generally, everyone can do, or can learn to do any of the jobs in the church, just as in the household. In some denominations, the exception might be those activities which are restricted to those who are ordained.

What needs to be done in most congregations?

In relation to worship

Family groups, men or women, church school classes from older elementary and older can do the job of ushering unless for some reason that job needs to be restricted. In one congregation, the ushers are also those who serve the communion; therefore, they must be on the board of deacons.

All people, including the very young, can be the assigned greeters. A family group assigned to greet gathering worshippers is appropriate if provision is made for those who are not 'traditional' family groups, like the single people in the congregation, to have ways of participating.

Choirs of people of different ages can provide special music. It is helpful if choirs know themselves to be contributors to worship rather than performers of great music. The music they provide may be great music. Their rendition of it may be faultless. But their attitude in providing it must be that they are worshippers along with the rest of the congregation, not performers entertaining an audience. Their location in the sanctuary might be decided on the basis of that place from which they can best contribute to the service of worship but also participate in it.

In many congregations, a sharing period during worship provides an opportunity in which visitors can be introduced, a brief witness to one's faith may be appropriate and announcements of special concerns and joys can be shared. In addition to the immediate value in such participation, sharing time also provides an opportunity for leadership development because people risk being visible and vocal in the group.

People of all ages can be involved in preparing the worship center, in folding the bulletins, in providing special music before or during the service, in delivering audio-tapes of the service to those unable to attend, and so on.

In relation to education programs

Those who might teach in the church school are more likely to respond to an invitation to do so if they are not expected to carry responsibility for the class alone, if they are provided with support structures, and if they know what is expected of them.

1. *Not being alone as a teacher*

Having more than one teacher with a group demonstrates the corporate dimension of our faith as Christians. Our styles of working with people need to demonstrate our interdependence with each other as well as our dependence on God.

Team teaching provides a structure into which people can learn to teach as Frank did in the story. Without a structure similar to the one described, Frank would likely not have become a teacher of children. He might have missed the three years of working with children that deepened his own faith as well as providing needed leadership with the group.

Monthly teachers' meetings are another way in which teachers can know that others are working together on a common task. The meetings can be designed to provide an occasion in which they can study as well as providing a chance to plan with others. Such a structure might be:

—content in some form: a brief lecture, a movie, a report of a book, sharing of an experience, and so on.

—opportunity to work with that content: discussion, open-ended stories, simulations and so on.

—then in groups with those working with people of similar ages, consider how that content relates to the group with which they work.

2. *Reasonable expectations*

Actions which the congregation can reasonably expect of all of the teachers might be that the person doing teaching of any group on behalf of the congregation would . . .

. . . worship with the congregation regularly,

. . . be on time at the assigned place,

. . . notify a specified person if they are unable to be present,

. . . use the material chosen by the group responsible for education in the congregation,

. . . participate in in-service meetings and training sessions,

. . . be willing to get more training in order to do the job in the best possible way.

The teachers can reasonably expect the congregation to . . .

. . . pray for them and the work they are doing,

. . . recognize the effort made by teachers through bulletin boards, items in newsletters or bulletins, formal recognition in public during the service of worship and through specially-designed thank-you ocassions,

. . . consecrate them to do the task of teaching on behalf of the congregation,

. . . provide resources, equipment and space adequate and appropriate to the situation,

. . . keep the facilities clean and pleasant,

. . . make available to them training sessions either in the congregation or in situations outside the congregation, such as denominational regional events or interdenominational ones.

3. *Term of service*

The term of service for teachers could vary with the situation. It is important that the term is clear. For those who work in the nursery with the very young, it might be possible that several people could take turns, with a new person starting every two weeks. In that way, always there would be a person not new to the children. Each person would work for four weeks. Both men and women should be recruited to be with the young children.

A schedule might look like:

        Mary—weeks 1-2-3-4
        Clyde—weeks   3-4-5-6

Ann — weeks   5-6-7-8
and so on.

People other than parents of the children should be recruited for the task of caring for the small ones. This serves two purposes: it symbolizes the responsibility of the whole congregation for the young in its midst and it relieves the parents for a brief time of the almost overwhelming experience of always being attentive to their children. It allows the parents the possibility of being with others in church school and worship and may be a factor that enables them to deal constructively with the crises of faith that are always present in every household but especially in those with young children.

In the congregation whose design for education was shared in Chapter Six, three two-member teams work on a schedule of two Sundays on and four Sundays off for the school year of September through June. This pattern is followed in the infant, toddler and preschool classes. In their classes for second and third through ninth to twelfth graders, teachers assume responsibility for one or more 12 to 14 week quarters for a calendar year.

With classes kindergarten through junior high, adults could be recruited to work for the school year of September through May or early June with other arrangements being made during the summer. At least two adults should be with every class regardless of class size. Both men and women should be with each class to provide models for both boys and girls of what it means to be faithful witnesses. It is better if the team is from more than one family. Children need the opportunity to get to know more adults in the congregation. Lasting relationships have developed between children and their teachers in the church school.

4. *Sharing responsibility*

With junior high school students, adults other than the church school teachers can be responsible for planning for social activities and situations in which the younger youth can work at some action programs. Those action programs may relate to and supplement the experiences of church school, but not necessarily so. The teachers of the church school class or classes can be expected to participate in social and action programs with the younger youth, but they ought not to have to plan for and manage such occasions.

Senior high youth and adults should have the opportunity to share in the choosing of their own leadership. This can be done in ways that not only allow them but also encourage them to plan for themselves and to take turns in leadership.

In one congregation, a young couple and a single young man were asked to share responsibility for being advisers of the senior high group. Then, other people in the congregation are asked to teach the group, depending on the subject matter, in units of from one to six sessions on subjects chosen by a youth committee. Such a pattern provides continuity of relationship with the group but also uses the special interests and abilitites of others, spreading the responsibility among more people in the congregation and not overburdening the three people with the on-going relationship.

CHAPTER TEN

Making Responsible Decisions

An Overview

Throughout this book, many illustrations and stories include ideas and concepts about decision-making and planning. After a brief general statement about decision-making and planning, the stories in this chapter describe people and situations in which decision-making and planning took place.

In the first story, a young woman considers her life-work and describes the process she used to arrive at a decision about that life-work. The process used by a family to decide to move is the focus of the next story. In it, one block to communication and to effective decision-making is obvious.

The other two stories come from congregational life. In the first, a group was called together specifically to make a critical decision. In the last story, a church board had to cope with pressure brought to bear on it by one man's action in the congregation.

All people make decisions. Quite often, we are not aware of the values we affirm and negate in the decisions we make. Some of our values are those which the culture gives us, almost without our knowing it is happening.

In spite of that reality, we can become more aware of more dimensions of our planning and decision-making. We can consider the contexts within which we must act. We can work together in ways that allow others to participate in the decision-making and planning, if it is appropriate in the given situation. We can take seriously our own lives and those of others by considering the future and moving into it with purpose instead of just drifting along into tomorrow, come what may.

The stories in this chapter are about decision-making and planning. They are not intended to illustrate any particular method of decision-making. The approach to planning used quite often depends on the situation. Think of some decisions you have made lately. On what basis did you decide? To what did you say YES, therefore saying NO to some other options? What do you hold as criteria for deciding between options available to you?

Many resources are available which provide guidance for doing planning. No one method is the most appropriate for every possible situation. In an article in the May 1980 "Educational Leadership" on lesson planning, a study is reported in which successful teachers were asked to list the planning decisions they made as they prepared their lessons. The method taught as the right one in classes at California State College, San Bernadino, requires students to learn and use a planning method that began with stating objectives. Only 43 percent of the 56 successful teachers reported that they first identified objectives to be taught. Another 30 percent looked first at the general area to be taught. The other 27 percent first assessed the needs of the students. All but one of those reporting included learning experiences or learning activities as one step in the planning sequence.

Throughout this book, many illustrations and stories include something about decision-making and planning. Contexts within which decisions are made were considered in the first section. Paying attention to the people involved in the work we do was treated in the second section. These stories focus directly on decision-making and planning.

Cindy was 20 years old and in her first year of pre-medical training at a small church college. She and her mother were asked to be co-leaders for a four-day experience for people involved in various dimensions of a denomination's education program. The theme for the event was planning for the future as an individual, a family member, and a professional educator.

In about the middle of the experience, the point had been reached for the group to make five-year timelines for themselves in relation to their personal, family and professional lives. It was decided that Cindy would lead this workshop and that she would share her own five-year timeline as an illustration of what the people should do.

She began by telling them that five years from that time she expected to be a student in a medical school of her choice, preparing to do family practice. She shared her opinion that those considering applicants for medical school were interested in academic ability but also in whether the person was serious about the intention to become a doctor. One way of demonstrating her seriousness, she thought, would be to have some recommendations of her work in various areas of medical work.

Her applications would be sent to five or six medical schools at the end of the summer two and a half years from the time the workshop was happening. She had three summers in which to do work as well as the possibility of using two more January inter-terms.

She already had the next summer's work tied down. She would be working as receptionist and office clerk for a doctor on the west side of Chicago. Most of his patients were blacks. On four nights a week, his office hours were from 6 p.m. until the office was empty. On the nights before he scheduled surgery two days a week, he did not have office hours.

She had already made inquiry about the possibility of working as a volunteer in a hospital in the mountains of Puerto Rico in some capacity during the second summer. She told the group that she intended in the third summer to do whatever kind of medically-related work she could find that would balance out her experience at that point.

Someone in the group asked her if doing such planning ahead did not limit her future too much. The question was raised about whether it might not be better to be free to do what came along.

Cindy's response was that having a direction for her life gave her criteria for accepting or refusing the opportunities that came along. She felt it gave her more freedom than less.

Cindy was a student in the medical school of her choice five years after that workshop. What actually happened to her was very close to what she had projected.

She began to work with the doctor in Chicago as planned. Halfway through the summer the office nurse quit, so the doctor taught Cindy to give injections, weigh babies, assist in minor operations and go on hospital rounds making notes for him.

The second summer in the hospital in Puerto Rico, she worked as an assistant in the emergency room. She learned to sew up machete cuts and to see how doctors and other personnel responded to the pressure of an emergency room.

She liked Puerto Rico and went back for a January inter-term the next year. This time she worked in hosptial records. She claimed at that point that the person who really kept a hospital together was the ward clerk who did all the paper work.

She had not lived with her family in the five years since they had *moved from Denver. She and her father agreed that it would be good for her to have an experience in white suburbia to balance what she had done thus far. He said it would also give her and the family a chance to get reacquainted since she would be living at home. She agreed.*

The job she found was working in the medical section of the state mental hospital located in the town. She began working as an assistant in the lab and as a notetaker for doctors as they made their rounds. She was a volunteer but kept regular hours and apparently did noticeably good work. Near the end of the summer, she was paid to do the blood chemistry and urinalysis tests for the two weeks that the lab technician was on vacation.

She made her applications to medical schools early that fall. It was no surprise to her to have an acceptance before Christmas and to have to decide among those who wanted her as a student.

Cindy's choice finally was a school in which family practice was regarded as a specialty, The other factor in her decision-making was that in the school she chose she found groups of students who were concerned with medical ethics—like a rape-victim advocacy group in which she became active.

Cindy had identified an issue—what should she do with her life professionally? She wanted to do something related to science. In addition to medicine, her initial interests also included marine biology. After she decided that being a doctor would provide her the opportunity of dealing directly with the hurt of the world, she then was able to define a goal for herself—getting into medical school.

Her next step was to consider factors involved in achieving that goal and to create plans that would deal with those factors. Being aware that she was a white, middle-class, young woman, she knew the world to have people in it different from herself. Her plans therefore needed to take account of the need to be in cultural situations different from that of her own.

Making the plans and even announcing them publicly as she did in the workshop, she still needed to take action to bring those plans to reality. She followed through with action, evaluated her actions and planned next steps at each decision-making point along the way.

Cindy obviously had a context within which she could make decisions. She had a dream. She acted to turn that dream into reality.

The job offer came in a telephone conversation on a Friday morning. Shirley had just returned from a weekday workshop and was heading from Denver to Rapid City for a weekend stint as a leader in a similar workshop. Then she would visit her parents in northern Wyoming before returning to Denver on Tuesday.

The phonecaller asked her if she would consider assuming responsibility for the education program of a denomination. She just laughed and said that she was contented where she was. She was teaching half-time in two seminaries and intended to move toward being full-time in the Roman Catholic one. So she laughed again and said that she was flattered to have been asked but, no, thank you.

The man on the other end of the phone line, who became her boss just over six months later, was a smart man. He told her it was a serious offer and he would not take an offhand answer, but would call back a week later for her response.

In the meantime, she ought to think seriously about the possibility. The church wanted someone with a background in education rather than someone from the parish. They also needed to have women on their staff who were married and willing to travel even when they had children at home. She told him that she would think about it.

She called her husband at his office and asked him how attached to his office he was. His was a firm doing mechanical enginering and it had grown to be fairly successful in the nearly fifteen years of its existence. There was a slight silence at the other end of the phone line as Earl tried to figure out what she was up to now. She told him of the job offer she had just received. He said that it was good to be wanted by the denomination and that they should talk about it when she got back to town next week.

On Tuesday, when she returned from the family visit, she was surprised that it was her husband rather than her son who picked her up at the airport in the middle of the day. He greeted her warmly. They talked family news until getting home for lunch. She fixed some soup and laid out things with which to make some sandwiches.

After a silent prayer of thanks for the meal, she asked, "Well?"

"We cannot do it, Shirley."

"Why not?" she asked.

Several days later, they were able to reconstruct that he had heard her questioning his judgment. She thought she was just asking for his process of reasoning.

One of his ways of dealing with conflict was to leave. That is what he did. That response always infuriated Shirley. She decided that this time she was not going to be the one to break the silence even if it meant a further strain in the marriage. She was angry.

So was Earl. He was able to maintain his silence and so was she. She talked with the younger members of the family, from sixth-grade Anita through grown-up John, and that year including an exchange student from France.

Four days later, on Friday, she was ready to call back the man who had phoned with the job offer to tell him that the family was not able to move at this time. As she started to walk toward the phone, she noticed a car pulling into the driveway. It was Earl, unexpectedly home in the middle of the day. She hurriedly moved back to the typewriter and began to type. That way she had her back to the door as he came in.

They had not spoken to each other for four days. He came in, walked over to her, put his hands on her shoulders and said that they had to talk about the situation.

Earl told her that Jerry, who had been working with him for ten years, had come to say that he was considering a job in Salt Lake City which would have him in a situation in which he would be more in control. The young man said that he had learned much from Earl but was now ready to be his own boss. Earl asked him to wait until Monday before making a final decision. Earl was then ready for the family to consider accepting the job offer made to Shirley. He was willing to look at the possibility of turning his engineering firm over to Jerry in order to be able to move with the family if the decision to move was made.

Then came the family decision-making time. John was not sure about the family leaving just at the time he was ready to get married. Cindy was concerned about having no place to call home during the year of study abroad into which she was headed the next year. Alan and Anita had friends they did not want to leave.

Shirley had the possibility of being the first woman to be a full-time teacher at the Roman Catholic seminary working in academic fields she loved. Earl wondered about what work he might do if he left his firm and whether it would survive without his presence.

The balance sheets were about equal for going and staying. Finally, Cindy asked about the family constitution which had been written sketchily a few years before. She remembered it saying something about the responsibility of the family to the church. The sheet was dug out of the file. It said:

HAVING DECIDED TO BE THE HECKMAN FAMILY
LIVING AT THIS TIME AND PLACE, WE COVENANT
TOGETHER THAT EACH WILL HONOR EACH AND
ALL FAMILY MEMBERS AND TAKE RESPONSIBILITY
FOR THE MAINTENANCE OF THE FAMILY IN ORDER

THAT THE CHURCH OF JESUS CHRIST THROUGH-
OUT THE WORLD BE RENEWED.

Only a little more conversation was necessary among the family members to arrive at the consensus that Shirley would be more likely to influence the development of congregations in the job offered than she would have as the visible outsider in the Roman Catholic seminary. It was decided that she would call the man with the job asking for more information.

He came to Denver to talk with Shirley and Earl about the job. Questions raised had to do with the individual and family lifestyles and about the commitment which Shirley had to the Ecumenical Institute (see note on page 165). He was able to reassure them about these issues. Weighing up all the balances, particularly the contribution they thought she would be able to make to the church through her work, it was decided that Shirley should accept the job offer.

The resident family included only Alan, Anita, Earl and Shirley when they moved that fall from Denver to Elgin. About fifteen months after they moved, Earl took a job as the head of the mechanical section of a very large sanitation engineering firm in Chicago.

The refusal to talk about issues is one of the blocks to responsible decision-making. Both Earl and Shirley used that route as a way to escape taking responsibility. After they finally decided to talk about it, the process the family moved through is obvious. They discerned negative and positive aspects to the proposed move to another place and another way of living. The issue was not whether Shirley would have a satisfying job to do. That was possible in either Denver or Elgin.

When the family members looked again at what they thought their mission to be, then they were able to make the decision in the light of that mission.

The committee appointed by the Nurture Commission to consider what church school material to use with the children was meeting with a staff person from the district office. The congregation had been using non-denominational material. At the suggestion of the district official, they were willing to look at some other possibilities.

After a time of prayer, the woman chairing the committee asked the district person to take over. His first question was, "What is important for seventh graders to know from their experience in the church before they reach junior high?" He asked each person to write down as many ideas, beliefs, concepts and stories as he or she could in the next five minutes.

After a couple of questions, the members of the group settled down to work.

The staff person then asked them to share two things from their individual lists as he began to make a group list on newsprint. When something was mentioned that someone else had already said, a check was made by the item previously listed. Soon the wall was covered with newsprint sheets. The process continued until everyone had shared all on each individual list.

Next, he asked them to share any other things that had come to mind during the group sharing. More items were listed. The members of the group expressed surprise at the number of things they expected children to have learned.

Because he knew well the material they were currently using, he and the people in the group were able to identify which of the things listed were dealt with in that material. He then took a marker of a different color and indicated which of the things left would be included in the materials recommended by the denomination.

Many of the items still left unchecked on the list were things like 'experiences with the congregation at worship' which were to be put on a separate list to be used as part of future planning.

The chairwoman then led the group to decide what they should recommend to the Nurture Commission about curriculum. After some discussion in which the district staff took no part, the group decided to report that the recommended materials should be used by the teachers for a six-month trial period. At that time, they would survey the teachers asking for their response to the material. Then they would consider again the question of what materials to use.

They also decided to report their whole list in the three categories to the Nurture Commission, asking that it might be shared with the congregation in some way. The people wanted to check whether their perceptions of what was needed to be learned was what others in the congregation thought also. They also asked that their third list of things that were not included in any materials might be used as a basis for evaluating the congregation's total program for children as well as for future planning of ways to help the desired things to happen.

Curriculum materials are sometimes seen as a problem in congregational education. Actually, the curriculum materials are only tools with which people can experience together something about being the community of Christian faith. If the teacher has a faith to share, he or she could use the Sears catalog or a newspaper as a means of sharing that faith. Materials can be chosen, though, that help the teacher in the faith-sharing task.

Materials of all kinds are available to those working in congregational education. It is a responsibility of those who work in national denominational offices to provide guidance about and access to resources that are consistent with the denomination's understandings and ways of operating. In the Church of the Brethren in recent years, the qualities desired in recommended materials have been the following:

(1) To be consistent with the understanding of the heritage of the Church of the Brethren, the material must have two focal points—right relationships with God and responsible participation in life with other human beings. Materials must take into account both of these dimensions. Many non-denominational materials deal only with right relationship with God and even do that as though it were a matter of private, personal faith. They often do not include responsible relationships with other humans beyond the individual's personal contacts.

(2) The material chosen must relate to the daily life of the participants. Our faith, Scripture and heritage as Christians cannot be understood as applying to times and places only in the past or in the future. The materials must deal with life here and now.

(3) Generally, the material must be denominational. Reasons for this are:

(a) We are assured that the material contains that part of our heritage that is concerned with our responsible relationship with other people. Much of the work related to easing human suffering around the world is done through denominational channels. That is part of what being a denomination means.

(b) The material must be that which encourages people to develop a commitment to the congregation and the work of the denomination beyond the congregation. The understanding about the church is that as a denomination, congregations can work together to accomplish decided-upon goals. Quite often, study about the church is left out of non-denominational materials.

(c) The materials chosen must be those which show the congregation as the center of the church. In the Church of the Brethren, a delegate body from congregations gathers to make decisions for the denomination.

(4) The materials chosen must be wholistic as possible. In words, pictures and images, people must be portrayed as the unique

human beings they are rather than as stereotypes. None of the images should diminish the glory of being human on the earth today or restrict the opportunity for people to have a full life. Some examples:

(a) The family must be portrayed as including other kinds of families in addition to the traditional image in which a father goes off to work every day and the mother stays home with their two children. Information about the kinds of families that might be in our congregations is included in Chapter Six.

(b) The resources must be those that do not include racial or cultural stereotypes. Ideas to be avoided are those like 'the poor are lazy' or 'if people would just work, they would have enough to eat.'

(c) Women must be seen as making a positive contribution. They must not be portrayed as subordinate to men or as second-class citizens with no place in the world of their own.

(d) Materials must reflect a global perspective. Many nondenominational materials deal with life as though the United States were the center of the universe. Such a nationalistic civil religion is not acceptable. The Lord is the center of the universe, we are not. The whole world that God created is our gift from God.

Donald was one of those people who are concerned about sharing the faith. He had been the evangelism conscience of the congregation for years, but without much response or support. He wanted to start a bus ministry but was not encouraged in that by others in the congregation. He talked about the bus ministry often to anyone who would listen. Finally he decided he needed to do something about it himself.

He had a small van that held several people. He began to go around his neighborhood, asking parents to let him take their boys to church school and worship with him. As this individual ministry got started, Donald brought three to five children each Sunday, though not always the same set of children.

He learned quickly which classes met in which rooms. Then during the service of worship, he and the children would sit right down front because that was where the children wanted to sit. The children had not had much experience with worship. They would talk with each other, stand up at the 'wrong' times, drop hymnals — all very normal behavior for children.

By the time the church board had its planning retreat in early September, Donald had been bringing the children every Sunday for several months. John, as chairman of the church board, was leading the work session of the board. He asked the group individually to list problems of the church. Then he asked them to share ideas from their individual lists in order to make a group list.

The first item mentioned was "Donald's children" to which there were several murmurs of assent. John responded by saying:

"I cannot put that on the list stated like that. Donald's children are just part of our situation. How can we talk about what problems we have in relation to the children he brings?"

"They are noisy during worship."

"They are irregular in attendance in the church school classes and so they do not know what we have been doing."

"We do not know their families."

"We do not know them."

By the time the retreat was over, the church had made plans that dealt with these problems and some of the others they had listed. Among those plans were:

— To deal with the noise of the children during the worship service, they decided that each week church board members would take turns having two of the children sitting with them. The children would not then be all together. This also allowed some of the people in the church to get to know the children better. It was also decided to begin having a children's story as a part of the service.

— To cope with the irregularity of the children, they decided to have a training session for the teachers to help them learn how to have each session complete in itself.

— To get to know the children and their families, they decided to begin again to share with the pastor in calling in homes. Including the families of Donald's children in the list of those for calls, they could begin to know them and their families.

In its planning, the church board identified problems that had developed through one man's independent actions. Then they were able to consider possible ways of responding to those problems. After that they were able to create some action plans that included the commitment of themselves to some action in the future.

One of the other dimensions of decision-making and planning is evident in this story. In order to sort out the complexity of a congregation or a household, we need to look at only one piece at a time. We cannot comprehend the whole all at once. As we lift out pieces or dimensions of life to examine, we create the impression that those pieces are separable or can be treated separately from the whole. That is not so. Any shift in one part of the whole brings about change in the other parts as well as to the whole. Donald's concern for evangelism affected the rest of the church's activities.

The total program of the congregation is strengthened when each part is consistent with the whole. For instance, the resources of the whole congregation are one of the limits within which all of the ministries and their activities must work. A balance of expenditure of resources, people and money by each ministry must be maintained that is consistent with what the congregation or household says it is intending to do. Here, as in the Heckman family move, the guideline is the understanding about the mission or goal of the group trying to make the decision.

Live Out the Promise

In all of these stories about decision-making, plans were made that projected over a period of time. Someone in each of the stories was operating out of a dream or vision about the way life could be. Our decision-making and planning is always done out of the context of what is important to us, what we intend the world to be and what we hope to do with our lives.

Those of us who call ourselves Christians share dreams about what life will be like when God's reign is acknowledged by all on earth. We have visions about what it might mean to be those who live with others so they can maintain their linkage with the past, anticipate the future, and participate responsibly in the present. We find it difficult, though, to grasp the reality of visions and dreams that may not materialize within our own lifetimes.

Science fiction provides images about time and space that can set free our creativity and our energy to work now for that which may come for future generations. The Dune trilogy by Frank Herbert is only one of many examples of such ideas in science fiction.

To most who saw the desert on the planet Dune, it was a wasteland in which nobody but a few tough people could live. But Pardot Kynes, the planetologist, had a dream that one day the desert would bloom. His whole being for all of his life was aimed at bringing that dream to reality.

Others tried to block him in his work. He figured out ways to get around the restrictions placed on him. He taught his son and the other children to be ecologically literate and very patient. He trained them to think and respond differently to their situation than others before them had.

When he was asked how long it would take for the transformation toward which he was working to take place, he answered that it would be from three hundred to five hundred years. He said that the thing would not come in the lifetime of any now living, nor in the lifetimes of their grandchildren three times removed, but it would come. Until then the work must continue: the digging, the building, the planting, the training of the children.

The work we do in the church will never be completed—at least, not in the lifetime of any person now living. The vision of the earth as a human habitation in which each one can sit 'neath a vine and fig tree at peace and unafraid, has been with us for thousands of years now.

Our decisions as individuals, as households, as congregations are based in our dreams and visions about what the world can be. My dream these days can be set forth in the style of that great dreamer, Martin Luther King, Jr.:

For I, too, have a dream.
It is a dream deeply rooted in the Christian faith.
I have a dream that one day the church will rise up and live
  out the true meaning of its gospel—love of God
  and neighbor as they confront us in Jesus Christ.
I have a dream that one day all people everywhere will have
  the possibility of living fully human lives.
I have a dream that the Christian church through its
  congregations around the world will have been an effective
  agent in bringing to reality that possibility.
This is the faith out of which I work.
Together with a faith like this, we shall be able to hue
  out of the reality given to us as a gift by God a
  new church that will enable that new world to be.
With this faith, we will be able to work together, to
  pray together, to struggle together, to do whatever is
  necessary together, knowing that love and justice
  will triumph.
With this faith, we will be able to share out of our
  abundance of the world's goods with those who starve
  and die because we know that the death of any human
  on earth diminishes us all.

ACKNOWLEDGMENTS

Thanks to those without whom the book would not have been written . . .

. . . my mother, my husband and the rest of the Heckman family who were willing, though not eager, that I tell stories about our life and our lives. It is a joke among us that I remember differently than any of them do. They have read the stories and agreed to let them be printed. Special thanks to Anita Heckman whose drawings of people enliven the pages of Chapter Six.

. . . my colleagues, with whom I have worked in the church, for their love, concern, encouragement and teaching; with special appreciation for Ralph McFadden, Robert Neff, Clarence Snelling, Harold Viehman, Iva Wonn, and D. Campbell Wyckoff.

. . . The Brethren Press for inviting me to write a book and to Fred Swartz for his editing of it.

. . . The Ecumenical Institute.* Anyone who knows the Ecumenical Institute will recognize that my thinking and ideas have been influenced greatly by my continuing involvement with the Institute.

Shirley J. Heckman

August 1980

*The purpose of the Ecumenical Institute (EI) is to serve the church. Its programs express and promote the awakening and renewal of the congregations and academic institutions of the church by providing a full curriculum of religious and cultural studies to equip individuals and groups to make responsible decisions.

The Ecumenical Institute came into being in 1962 when the Church Federation of Chicago assumed responsibility for the Evanston Institute for Ecumenical Studies. The Institute had been founded by a group of Chicago businessmen out of a resolution passed at the 1954 meeting of the World Council of Churches in Evanston, Illinois. The Federation invited Dr. Joseph Wesley Mathews of the Christian Faith-and-Life Community at the University of Texas at Austin to become the Dean of the Ecumenical Institute.

Seven families with whom Dr. Mathews worked decided also to join the staff of the Institute as teaching faculty without compensation. The staff began to model itself after historical 'third' orders — family orders, becoming what is now called The Order: Ecumenical. The Order continues to provide training and research staff for Institute programs. It is self-supporting through income earned by its membership and contributed to a common pool of income. The fund provides total care of Institute staff, including health, education and annuity funds.

In 1963, the Institute and its seven staff families moved from Evanston to a sixteen-block area on Chicago's west side which became known as Fifth City. The work in Fifth City was an experiment in comprehensive community development, which became a base for work around the world through the program division called the Institute of Cultural Affairs (ICA). The purpose of ICA, formally incorporated in 1973, is to develop and demonstrate effective methods of comprehensive local renewal and to motivate the spirit of responsibility and cooperative action.

From the seven original families, the staff by 1978 grew to more than 1500 people in 100 staff locations in 32 nations, in each of which is a national board of directors. A large percentage of the new staff is indigenous to the various nations where the Institute provides its programs. Coordination centers have been established in Brussels, Hong Kong, Bombay and Singapore in addition to that in Chicago.

For more information about the work of the Ecumenical Institute, write to 4750 North Sheridan Road, Chicago, Illinois, 60640, or phone 312-769-6363. Indicating that you read about the Institute in this book would be appreciated.